Basic Care for
NATURALLY TEXTURED

HAIR

Basic Care for

NATURALLY TEXTURED

HAIR

Cultivating Curly, Coily, and Kinky Hair

Diane Carol **Bailey**

Angelo P. **Thrower, MD**

DELMAR

THOMSON LEARNING

Australia   Canada   Mexico   Singapore   Spain   United Kingdom   United States

PERSONAL CARE COLLECTION

NOTICE TO THE READER

Delmar Staff:

Business Unit Director: Susan L. Simpfenderfer
Executive Editor: Marlene McHugh Pratt
Acquisitions Editor: Paul Drougas
Developmental Editor: Patricia A. Gillivan
Editorial Assistant: Rebecca McCarthy
Executive Marketing Manager: Donna J. Lewis
Channel Manager: Wendy E. Mapstone
Executive Production Manager: Wendy A. Troeger

For more information, contact Delmar, 3 Columbia Circle, PO Box 15015, Albany, NY 12212-0515; or find us on the World Wide Web at http://www.delmar.com

International Division List

Asia:
Thomson Learning
60 Albert Street, #15-01
Albert Complex
Singapore 189969
Tel: 65 336 6411
Fax: 65 336 7411
Japan:
Thomson Learning
Palaceside Building 5F
1-1-1 Hitotsubashi, Chiyoda-ku
Tokyo 100 0003 Japan
Tel: 813 5218 6544
Fax: 813 5218 6551
Australia/New Zealand:
Nelson/Thomson Learning
102 Dodds Street
South Melbourne, Victoria 3205
Australia
Tel: 61 39 685 4111
Fax: 61 39 685 4199

UK/Europe/Middle East:
Thomson Learning
Berkshire House
168-173 High Holborn
London
WC1V 7AA United Kingdom
Tel: 44 171 497 1422
Fax: 44 171 497 1426

Thomas Nelson & Sons LTD
Nelson House
Mayfield Road
Walton-on-Thames
KT 12 5PL United Kingdom
Tel: 44 1932 2522111
Fax: 44 1932 246574

Latin America:
Thomson Learning
Seneca, 53
Colonia Polanco
11560 Mexico D.F. Mexico
Tel: 525-281-2906
Fax: 525-281-2656
South Africa:
Thomson Learning
Zonnebloem Building
Constantia Square
526 Sixteenth Road
P.O. Box 2459
Halfway House, 1685
South Africa
Tel: 27 11 805 4819
Fax: 27 11 805 3648

Canada:
Nelson/Thomson Learning
1120 Birchmount Road
Scarborough, Ontario
Canada M1K 5G4
Tel: 416-752-9100
Fax: 416-752-8102
Spain:
Thomson Learning
Calle Magallanes, 25
28015-MADRID
ESPANA
Tel: 34 91 446 33 50
Fax: 34 91 445 62 18
International Headquarters:
Thomson Learning
International Division
290 Harbor Drive, 2nd Floor
Stamford, CT 06902-7477
Tel: 203-969-8700
Fax: 203-969-8751

Library of Congress Cataloging-in-Publication Data
Bailey, Diane Carol.
   Basic care for naturally textured hair : cultivating curly, coily, and kinky hair / Diane
Carol Bailey, Angelo P. Thrower.
      p. cm.—(Personal care collection)
   ISBN 0-7668-3761-0
      1. Hairdressing of Blacks. 2. Hair—Care and hygiene. 3. Hairstyles. I. Title: Naturally
textured hair. II. Thrower, Angelo P. III. Title. IV. Series.
TT972 .B347 2001

646.7'24—dc21

2001037235

Contents

Roots—
Locks 'Round the Clock

According to a French historian, the first haircut was done by draping hair across a rock and using a stone to hack it off. The effect must have looked worse than a cut done with pinking shears, although beauty is always in the eye of the beholder. It could be considered the first textured style or shag. At any rate, flaked stone tools, which could have been used for cutting, date back to the Middle Paleolithic period, from 100,000 B.C. to 35,000 B.C.

AFRICAN INNOVATIONS

The first highly decorative hairstyles were noted among African tribes, which used hair to make important social and cultural statements. Often, specific styles of braiding indicated whether a woman was single, in mourning, celebrating the birth of her first child, or was of high social rank. In some tribes, hair length was a measure of strength; in others, cutting the hair was a way of driving out evil spirits, which were thought to enter the body through the hair.

Many tribes were and still are identified by their distinctive hairstyles. Women of the Masai tribe of Kenya wind their hair into an elaborate bob. The Zulus set highly unusual styles in place with the aid of mud. Many other tribes still create twisted ringlets, plaits, and locks, using various types and colors of clay.

Throughout history, asymmetrical cuts were used to indicate age or profession. The royal runners of the Dahomey Empire shaved one side of the head and carefully shaped the opposite into a fuller style. In Egypt, barbers created a "Horus lock," which was a long lock left to fall over one ear, signifying youth.

ANCIENT EGYPTIAN STYLES

Hairstyles—and the cosmetology profession—were well documented by scribes of ancient Egypt. For almost 3000 years, style changes in Egypt were minimal. The women of Egypt wore extremely elaborate plaiting, which was decorated with shells, sequins, and glass, or gold beads. Particular styles were a sign of social status, and the average citizen would never wear the same style as the queen, unless she was prepared to lose it, along with her head. Between 3000 and 1596 B.C., the

Egyptians moved from wearing braided styles to favoring wigs. Men invariably shaved their heads and wore wigs; women cut their hair very short and wore wigs made of human hair or sheep's wool, because it was closest to their natural texture. Flax or palm fiber were also used to create wigs, and examples were found in early tombs.

The cosmetology trade had its own hierarchy in Egypt. Barbers for the wealthy visited clients in their homes each morning and attended to their styling needs, as well as to their nails. It is notable that barbers were sometimes doctors, a tradition that continued well into the tenth century, when French barber-surgeons joined to form their own organization. Traveling barbers, who were primarily patronized by the poor, sat under trees waiting for passersby to become clients. Anointing the hair with essential oils, such as sandalwood and frankincense, was an important part of dressing locks.

Egyptians were clean shaven or wore fake, decorated beards, but the first formal record of shaving is found among the Romans in the fourth century B.C. Alexander the Great is credited with introducing the trend; supposedly he was afraid that during hand-to-hand combat, his men could be seized by their beards. Later beards became a sign of high social position, until the emperor Constantine brought back shaving, around the fourth century A.D.

Henna was used to color hair—as were berry juices. Both also served as cosmetics. Indeed, an excellent argument could be made that ancient Egypt was the birthplace of the true art of cosmetology. It is also said that Egyptian women bathed in sour milk; milk is a source of alpha hydroxy acids, which are much touted in skin care today.

The women of Morocco and the Middle East also used henna, in a highly unique fashion. In what may be the first form of tattooing, women created elaborate and stunningly beautiful designs using various shades of henna, which stained the skin and nails. Frequently this ancient art was part of a marriage ritual, and it can still be seen today.

ARCHAEOLOGICAL EVIDENCE

Throughout the world, ancient paintings and scrolls show that hairstyles were almost always a measure of social status. Painted ceilings in palaces on the island of Crete provide further insight into the ancient art of hairdressing. The Cretans, who lived around 2000 B.C. to 1400 B.C., had thick, dark hair that was either naturally curly or artificially curled and waved. Many ancient peoples were familiar with oils, waxes, and unguents, and the Cretans used them to set their hair into structured waves and curls. More elaborate hairstyles were worn at the court; the poor wore simplified versions of those styles. Waxes and oils were also used in ancient Persia to create curls.

In India, which boasts one of the oldest civilizations in the world, oral tradition took precedence over writing until about 1200 B.C., but ancient paintings can be seen that depict women in long, heavy braids.

Perhaps the oldest hairstyle that was not a wig that was ever seen firsthand by archaeologists is braids, which were noted on mummies found in China. The mummies were astonishingly well preserved, because they were found in the northwest foothills and the fringes of the Taklimakan Desert, where daytime temperatures soar above 100 degrees.

Whereas Egyptian mummies are older, few retained their real hair, and they were often found wearing wigs. The Chinese mummies were an important find, because they appeared almost exactly as the people did in real life. Surprisingly, they were not of Chinese descent, but were blonde and light-brown-haired Caucasians, who could have traveled from Europe or the Ukraine. All the women wore several long braids, and a child wore a tattoo on her wrist. Resting with them were wooden combs. However, these relatively simple braids were nothing like the astonishing works of art found in early African civilizations.

Heated tools were used to style hair as early as the fifth or fourth century B.C. A glazed brick relief piece of art, which is displayed at the Louvre in Paris today, depicts Susa warriors from Iran (Persia) with curly hair and beards. Historians surmise that the perfectly shaped curls were created with hot tongs, probably heated over a flame.

HAIRCOLOR HISTORY

Haircolor has its own colorful history. African tribes used red ochre and animal fat to color their hair; some say that one of the earliest formulas for covering gray hair was an African one that used bull's blood cooked in oil.

It is believed that in 27 B.C., the Gauls dyed their hair red to indicate class rank. At this time there were no natural redheads in existence, at least that were ever depicted or documented.

The first documented natural redhead appeared in Scotland during the Dark Ages. Scientists believe that it was a genetic mistake. Because of red's surprising appearance—and its unfortunate timing—the haircolor became associated with witchcraft.

Blonde, on the other hand, was noted much earlier in history. How did blondes get their reputation for having more fun? Roman law decreed that yellow or blonde was to be worn by "women of the night." Later, during the Renaissance, women favored golden hues and considered them angelic. They enhanced blonde shades by mixing black sulfur, alum, and honey, applying it to their hair, and spreading their tresses over a brimless hat until the sun helped them achieve the desired shade. Centuries later, Hollywood restored blondes' reputation as the bad girls of society, or at least as its sex symbols.

After the Year Zero

The Anastazi, who lived in prehistoric times and developed basket making and agricultural techniques as early as 100 A.D., are now extinct, although the adobe houses they lived in around 700 A.D. can still be seen in the Southwest. Evidence shows that they, too, favored braids. After the Anastazi disappeared, certain Native American tribes shaved their hair into fierce-looking Mohawks, imitated in recent times by punk rockers. Many used feathers in elaborate headdresses or to adorn simple styles.

Like many groups, Native Americans discovered that the way they wore their hair, which emphasized cultural pride, caused strong reactions in Europeans. Hair became something to fear, both because it was different and because it was seen as a refusal to give up the past, or assimilate. As any student of history knows, the easiest way to suppress a population is to deny them their history and their culture.

The wearing of Native-American and other cultural hairstyles brought about discriminatory acts, such as expulsion from school, as recently as the early 1970s; African-American women were dismissed from jobs around the same time for wearing traditional African braids. The Afro became a political statement, which also brought about strong reactions. In 1967, a member of the Afro American Students Union at the University of California told a white reporter from the *New York Times,* "We decided to stop hating ourselves, trying to look like you . . . straightening our hair."

According to the *Encyclopedia of Pop Culture,* the Afro lost favor when non-blacks began wearing it. Art Garfunkel's hair was called an "Isro" (a reference to his Jewish/Israeli heritage), and non-Jewish whites who wore their hair full and curly called the style an "Anglo." Interestingly, the *Encyclopedia of Pop Culture* also notes that in the 1970s, the government of Tanzania in Africa outlawed Afros because they had become an "emblem of western cultural colonialism, favored by fashion-conscious members of Tanzania's decadent elite."

Even today, African Americans who embrace the ancient tradition of hairlocking and proudly wear a style that has been often called "dreadlocks," and is now respected as "African locks," are discovering that discrimination in employment is still a real and present threat.

But the suppression, acceptance, and frequent mainstream adaptation of various cultural hairstyles occurred over hundreds of years. During that time, African Americans in particular adapted unique ways of dealing with the situation. The techniques they developed are used today to style curly hair.

Early Development of Modern American Hairstyles and Techniques

When African slaves were brought to the United States and South America (most notably, Brazil, which imported more slaves than any other country), they left their elaborate wood and ivory combs behind. Without combs, shampoos, or scissors, they felt they had little choice but to cover their heads in rags or hack off their hair as best as they could, close to the head. The only shears available were those used for sheep and other animals.

Scalp disease and hair damage were prevalent. Sometimes cornmeal was used to clean dirt and oil from the hair, and lard was used in an attempt to protect and soothe the scalp. Sometimes kerosene was rubbed through the hair with rags, or sulfur was used.

One of the earliest methods for straightening hair involved heating a piece of flannel over an open fire, oiling the hair with lard, and pulling strands of hair through the hot flannel. Knowledge of braiding techniques survived, and sometimes hair was braided up, under the rags that were used to cover the hair and protect it from the follies of working in cotton fields.

Cultural Segregation

Around this time, the Chinese, who often wore their hair in long pigtails, were used as cheap labor to build the railroads. Between 1848, when the United States acquired California, and 1869, when the transcontinental railroad was completed, Chinese immigrants, who were not permitted to become citizens, were frequently harassed because of their hair. Westerners, who had heard the Chinese believed that they could not get into "heaven" if their pigtails were cut off (never mind that Shintoists and Buddhists do not believe in "heaven"), would cut off their long braids as cruel sport. In 1882, the Chinese Exclusion Act prevented immigration; later quotas were established, which were not eliminated until 1965. Because of this, Asian beauty care became segregated and was frequently a home-care situation, just as it was for Africans.

After the Civil War ended in 1865, former slaves turned to blacksmith's tools, which were heated at the kitchen stove or fireplace and used as crude straightening irons. Thus the birth of the kitchen or home hairdresser came about. Later blacks began to open their own salons and barber shops. Needless to say, they could not patronize "white" salons, and Caucasian hairdressers had neither the desire nor the education to service non-Caucasian clients.

The Development of Products for Curly Hair

Early products used by former-slave barbers were fats, oils, and petroleum products. From the turn of the century through the 1950s, the emphasis was on forcing curly hair into a straight configuration. Hair growers and straighteners were introduced in the early 1900s. Many African Americans created their own products, selling concoctions that were developed on kitchen stoves from door to door.

Early Pioneers

Pierre Toussaint, a Haitian-born barber who died in 1853, was recently exhumed from his resting place in a lower Manhattan cemetery, and there is talk about making him a saint. Supposedly, Toussaint's owner freed him (at an unusually early date), but he stayed on to care for his impoverished former owner's widow, supporting her with his hairdressing trade. Barclay Street, where he was buried, was renamed Pierre Toussaint Square; shortly after that, Pierre Toussaint Shampoo turned up at a nearby East Village shop, Little Ricky's.

During Reconstruction, barbershops became the place where men congregated to share news and exchange ideas. For many former slaves, who were just learning to read, barbershop conversations were the primary source of information. African-American beauty schools sprang up and often doubled as social centers. Some served as hotels because blacks were not permitted to stay elsewhere in town.

Throughout this time, many pioneers in beauty culture emerged. Detroit-based historian Vernice Mark provided much of the following information on these early African-American trailblazers.

ANNIE TURNBO POPE MALONE

One school that served as a center of social activity was Poro College, established in St. Louis by Annie Turnbo Pope Malone. Around 1900, Annie, who had never finished high school, began to study chemistry and developed a product called "Wonderful Hair Grower." In 1906, she copyrighted the trade name "Poro," adapting the slogan, "It Blazes the Trail and Still It Leads."

She traveled throughout the South, promoting her product, settled in St. Louis, and began to train young girls in the beauty field. If the girls stayed with her for five years, they received a diamond ring.

By 1918, she moved into the building that became known as Poro College, at the corner of St. Ferdinand and Pendleton Avenues. Poro College grew to hold classrooms, barbershops, and a dormitory. At the height of the school's success, Mrs. Malone employed 175 people in the beauty trade, and in 1924, she traveled to Europe to study beauty culture techniques and methods in those countries.

Throughout her life, she gave monetary gifts to a variety of institutions, and in 1945, the St. Louis Orphan's Home Building Fund named its home the Annie Malone Children's Home, honoring her for a 10,000 dollar bestowment.

Chuck Berry was one of the many graduates of the St. Louis Poro School of Beauty Culture. He might have been a great cosmetician, but when he was brought to Chess Records in 1955 by Muddy Waters, he turned an old fiddle tune called "Ida Red" into "Maybellene," and a legend was born. Although many think Maybellene referred to his beauty-school background, Berry once told a reporter that, as a child, he had known a cow by that name. (Poro College no longer exists, but its name lives on in the Poro Beauty Salon in St. Louis.)

MADAME C. J. WALKER

Whereas many African-American barbershops created their own hair oils and products, the most well-known pioneer of hair-care products exclusively for African Americans is Madame C. J. Walker. Born in 1867, in Delta, Louisiana, Sarah Breedlove was orphaned at seven, married at fourteen, and widowed at twenty. Sarah McWilliams then married Charles J. Walker, and spent much of her early life as a laundress, earning $1.50 a day. She began developing hair-care products and selling them door to door around 1910, and she developed a straightening comb that replaced pull tongs, which she sold along with a hair-growth formula. *Hair growth* is a misleading term; most of these formulations "stretched" the hair, making it appear longer and straighter.

Madame Walker moved her office from city to city and formally established a company in 1911. She continued to expand her line, offering "Tetter Salve," a scalp-treatment product, and opening a beauty school. She produced the first line of cosmetics for black women and eventually employed hundreds of salespeople. The newsletter that she produced for her sales force included sales tips and a column entitled "Concentrated Wisdom," which provided personal inspirations such as, "Aim for your goal, " and "To improve yourself, improve by example." She even authored an instructional book, in which a chapter on bobbed hair recommends that you cut the style to suit the patron's features. It may be the first reference to individualizing a haircut.

Throughout the years, she continued to develop her product line and her system of beauty culture education. The "Walker System" eventually came to be taught in Madame C. J. Walker Colleges, located in several cities.

Always keeping control of her company and her money, Madame Walker eventually built a half-million-dollar mansion in Irvington-on-the-Hudson, New York. Her friend, the great singer Enrico Caruso, named it "Villa Lewaro," for her daughter, Lelia Walker Robinson. It was supposedly furnished for an amount in excess of 350,000 dollars—a virtual fortune at the time.

When Madame C. J. Walker died in 1919, she was eulogized as the richest woman of her race, and many called her the first black millionaire. Her daughter sold Villa Lewaro in 1930, but the company Madame Walker established continued throughout the 1960s, offering over seventy-five different products at its pinnacle.

SARAH SPENCER WASHINGTON

Sarah Spencer Washington was born some twenty-six years after the Emancipation Proclamation, and around 1914, began her career in beauty culture. She graduated from Norfolk Mission College, studied beauty culture in York, Pennsylvania, and went on to study chemistry at Columbia University. Better prepared educationally than Madame Walker or Annie Malone, she made her mark helping scores of African-American women find financial independence as beauticians.

In 1918, she established her business in Atlantic City, New Jersey, teaching beauty culture during the day and selling her own products at night. Her company, Apex News and Hair Company, used groups of agents, who demonstrated and sold her products. It became the foundation for Apex schools. These schools, which eventually dotted the nation coast to coast, graduated thousands of new cosmeticians. Even today, many tell the story of how Madame Washington, as she came to be known, refused to purchase machinery to increase production during the depression, opting instead to retain hundreds of workers who performed tasks manually.

THE NATIONAL BEAUTY CULTURE LEAGUE

One of the oldest and most prestigious beauty organizations in the world is the National Beauty Culturists League (NBLC). Organized on October 1, 1919, in Philadelphia, by R. V. Randolph, S. L. Latimer, E. R. Cargel, M. Paris, and B. Tolliver, it was incorporated in 1920 under the laws of the State of Delaware. It was established to further beauty education, advance high standards of conduct, seek beneficial legislation, and unify African-American hairdressers.

In 1944, at the NBLC convention in Philadelphia, the National Institute of Cosmetology was established to provide intensive education prior to the convention. Cordelia Greene Johnson founded the institute. Twenty-four students attended the first session in 1944; in 1976, in the Bahamas, 802 students attended.

Throughout the years, the NBLC fought to eliminate segregation on boards of beauty control, provided scholarships to hundreds of aspirants, and continued to advance the causes of African-American hairdressers. Today the Institute and the NBLC, headquartered in Washington, D.C., offer annual five-day intensive workshops, a university extension program, and a doctoral program with college credits. It is the only known organization offering a doctorate in the profession; it is also the oldest beauticians' and cosmetologists' organization in the United States.

Hair Straightening

During the 1920s, 1930s, and 1940s, pressing the hair with a "straightening comb" or pull tongs became a biweekly ritual in African-American homes. Press and curl techniques permitted a variety of styles, including marcel or finger waves, upsweeps, French rolls, chignons, Dutch bobs, pompadours, and ponytails. Caucasians, who once sat in a tortuous perm machine enduring the smoking and burning of the equipment, switched to the cold wave, which was introduced by the Zotos Corporation in the 1930s.

The 1940s marked the advent of early chemical hair straighteners. During this time, the primary method for straightening hair was to use lye, and it was men, not women, who used the products. The lye was mixed with water and an egg to dissolve the lye crystals and create a thick mixture that could be applied to the hair. Often white potato flour was added in an attempt to cut the burning, but scalp burns and hair loss were still a frequent result. The movie *Malcolm X* portrays this painful process realistically, emphasizing the agonizing wait to remove the product. Early straightened styles were called "konked" hair, and one early straightening product was called "Konkaleen."

Through the early 1940s, hair preparations continued to be kitchen brews that had varying measures of efficacy. When finger waves came into style, the stylist or barber had to mold in "memory waves" while the lye product did its work. This definitely demanded gloves, yet some did not use them, in deference to the client, who suffered through the process. Roger Simon, who perfected the early konk finger-wave process, went on to marry Ethel Waters and open a barbershop with comedian Redd Foxx in the 1970s.

Today's Pioneers

In 1946, Nathaniel Bronner Sr. formed Bronner Brothers in Atlanta, Georgia. His sister had opened a beauty shop in 1937, and Bronner started selling Apex hair oil, which he took along on his paper route. Today the company has diversified, with beauty supply stores, innumerable products, the Cottonwood Spa and Motel in Cottonwood, Alabama, and *Upscale* magazine, which enjoys national distribution.

In the 1950s, commercial hair straighteners were introduced to permanently straighten curly hair. These greatly improved relaxers made it possible for an even greater variety of styles.

Hispanic and Latino men sometimes used similar preparations as those used by African Americans to create the slicked-back looks seen at the height of Mambo days. Later, Brylcreem, Vitalis, and Wildroot were used to weigh the hair down and keep it back when possible. These three products, more than any other, gave birth to the term "greasers," which was used to label boys with slicked back hair and wild lifestyles, who imitated Elvis Presley.

Hispanic Home Styles

Like African Americans, Hispanics found that there were no products in the mainstream market that met their needs. They developed a variety of creative home-brewed treatments—many of which are now making a resurgence with the return to "natural" and herbal-based products. While during the 1940s and 1950s there were barbershops for men, women turned to home hairdressers, who spoke Spanish and understood their beauty demands. Cubans, Dominicans, and Puerto Ricans, who entered the United States in large numbers at somewhat different times, worked within their own communities. Cubans, who left their country during Castro's rise to power and frequently settled in Miami, often hid their jewels in their hair to get them out of the country.

The products used and home remedies created were sometimes based on country of origin. However, many different groups of Hispanics arrived at the same solutions. Balmer Galindez, who conducted original research for this book, interviewed many Spanish-speaking stylists who reported that through the 1960s, Hispanics used techniques that were developed decades earlier. Their ingenuity, creativity, and determination to have their beauty needs met is evident in the innovative techniques that he discovered.

Relaxers were made using lye, potassium, and soap shavings. First the lye was boiled and set to cool. Then soap shavings were added, along with extracted potato juice, which was intended to make the formula gentler and prevent scalp burns. Petroleum was used to base the scalp before the mixture was applied. Other relaxer additives, such as cinnamon sticks, were intended to strengthen the hair. Another hair strengthener was created by boiling the sole of a shoe. The water was used in a relaxer formula or was used alone as a hair treatment.

To create a vibrant haircolor, the bark of the mahogany tree was boiled and mixed with chamomile, cinnamon, and an herb called "campeche." For the client who wanted her hair bleached, bleach was made with straight potassium, soap shavings, and peroxide. The mixture was extremely strong and required a two-day wait before toning, lest scalp burns result.

Hair was often hot combed; when it was roller set for control, it required the use of a setting lotion. Just a few included a gelatin and water mixture, a mixture of sugar and water, or the application of beer that had been allowed to go flat overnight. The hair was set in small sections and wrapped around long, torn strips of paper bag. This technique created ringlets made popular by child star Shirley Temple and was popular with children.

To straighten hair or make a set last longer, the setting lotion was applied and hair was wrapped around an emptied, washed can that once held tomato juice. Both ends of the can were removed, and it was held in place with bobby pins. The hair was covered under a silk scarf until the cans could be removed. Pin curls and finger waves were also popular options.

With harsh lyes being used, hair condition was an important beauty issue. Home conditioners used by Hispanic hairdressers are still recommended by consumer beauty magazines in all markets today. These include olive oil mixed with herbs; coconut oil, which was created by frying the meat of the coconut until only oil remained; mashed and strained avocados; and whipped eggs.

RELAXERS IMPROVE

Among the first companies to perfect the relaxer were Summit Laboratories, founded in 1959 by three entrepreneurs, and Johnson products, founded by George E. Johnson in 1954. Johnson had previously worked for the Fuller Products Company, another entrepreneurial, African-American-owned company. Throughout the 1980s, the company flourished, but in the early 1990s, Johnson and his wife, who had helped build the company from inception, divorced, and the company changed forever. Johnson Products was the first black-owned company to trade on the stock exchange.

Products and Pride Lead to New—and Rediscovered—Styles

During the 1960s, which were the Motown years, singers such as the Supremes influenced hairstyles with their bouffants, flips, teased tops, and pageboys. Wigs and falls became popular, and many African-American women used them to achieve longer hair.

Although relaxed hair dominated the market for a time, the Afro usurped it during its popularity, which rose in the mid to late 1960s. In the late 1970s, extension braids became an alternative to the Afro. Cornrows, naturals, African locks, relaxed styles, and press and curls were all achievable style alternatives. Then the curly perm was born.

The perfected cold wave process allowed curly hair to be retexturized or rearranged to simulate soft curls. When the Jheri curl appeared, the product name came to stand for the style.

Although new product formulations and chemicals allowed clients with curly hair to experience a range of looks, it was not until the late 1980s that men and women of all backgrounds began wearing a vast range of styles. Caucasians abandoned the nightly torture of setting hair on the pink plastic or brush rollers that dominated the 1950s and 1960s; the long, straight styles and perms of the 1970s became more diverse. For African Americans, wearing a relaxed style was no longer considered trying to "look white," any more than a Caucasian wearing a perm was trying to "look black." "Cookie-cutter" or stamped-out, identical looks were disappearing.

NATURAL HAIRSTYLES

Wearing hair that took advantage of its natural texture also became popular. Native Americans began wearing traditional ornamentation—without expulsion from schools; Puerto Rican and other Hispanic women began to enjoy their naturally curly locks without subduing them via roller sets. In the late 1970s, braided styles reappeared and have grown in popularity ever since. Most are based on the ancient art of cornrowing, which is called *canerowing* by West Indians. In modern styles, the hair is either braided without hair additions, or human or synthetic hair is woven into the cornrows, or attached and braided on its own.

The art of cultivating natural locks also reappeared. For years, many associated locks with the "dreadlocks" worn by Rastafarians and West Indians, which are created by allowing the elements to have an effect on hair. But in the 1980s, ancient African techniques for creating cultivated locks reemerged, giving birth to a whole new professional title: locktician. Lockticians do not use hair additions, but guide curly hair through natural stages of growth until it permanently locks in place. In the modern spelling, *locks* often becomes *locs*.

MODERN DEVELOPMENTS

In 1981, the American Health and Beauty Aids Institute (AHBAI) was founded as a national association of black-owned companies that produce hair-care and cosmetic products for the black consumer. In response to African-American-owned companies losing 30 percent of market share in the 1980s to mass-market companies, the organization introduced the Proud Lady logo, which stands for membership in the organization and the goal of keeping black dollars in the black community.

Braiders and natural hairstylists, who had continued to pass down and perfect techniques from generation to generation, grew in numbers and popularity throughout the 1970s; in the 1980s, they began to demand the right to separate licensing. They became part of a cultural revival that rediscovered history, and today they are redefining African-American beauty.

Because natural hairstylists do not use chemicals and have a completely different philosophy about hair, many do not want to be constrained by cosmetology regulations, which were written in the 1930s. Licensing regulations that required graduation from a cosmetology school were intended to protect clients from improper chemical usage, and made no sense to the natural or "cultural hairstylist." In addition, cosmetology schools do not teach the braiding techniques that natural stylists need to know.

A DISTINCT AND SEPARATE PROFESSION

By the 1990s, states began to create separate specialty licenses for braiders, lockticians, and natural hairstylists, who deliver very different services from cosmetologists. Braiders in Washington, D.C., fought for separate licensing and won it after a ten-year political battle; licensing for natural hairstyling has also passed in New York. Although some believed that natural or cultural hairstylists should not be subjected to any licensing procedure, for others the license represents recognition of the profession and an upgrading of standards. It also permits the development of a separate curriculum that, at last, will teach what natural stylists need to know.

Today, braid artists, lockticians, and cultural hairstylists work out of their homes and in numerous salons across the United States, where the elaborate styles they create are astonishingly intricate works of beauty, much like the braids and locks of early African tribes. In fact, most of the techniques they use are based on almost-lost, rediscovered arts.

CHAPTER 2

Black Hair Care

Poets and writers have often referred to hair as "the crowning glory" of the human body. It is one of the most prominent appendages of the body, and quite possibly, the appendage given the most attention. In fact, though, hair has no particular function other than decoration, yet its care and styling generates and continues to support a multibillion-dollar industry.

Just as black skin requires special considerations in treatment and grooming, so does black hair. Black hair is naturally curly. It is also very prone to dryness, dullness, breakage, and scalp irritations. In addition, fast-changing fashion trends expose hair to many styles and products that can damage it. Therefore, black hair must be styled in certain ways and hair-care products specially formulated for black hair used.

Hair care is a growth industry and represents a multibillion-dollar market. The retail market for ethnic hair care products has reached as high as 1.7 billion dollars and is still on the rise. The majority of these products are sold to black consumers in the United States. Considering that African Americans make up only 12 percent of the population of the United States, the potential world market for ethnic hair care products is truly staggering. In Africa alone, for example, there are more than 650 million people. Numbers such as these require that skin care professionals as well as consumers have the knowledge necessary to choose the right products and to properly care for this psychologically vital appendage.

HAIR AND THE BODY

In humans, hair grows from below the skin everywhere on the body except on the palms of the hands and the soles of the feet. There are two types of hair—Vellus hair and terminal hair.

Vellus hair is also referred to as baby hair, although it grows on adults as well as children. It is very short, less than 30 microns in length; very fine, less than 40 microns in diameter; and hypopigmented, that is, colorless. Vellus hair grows virtually everywhere on the body in both women and men. Because of its extremely small length and diameter and lack of coloration, however, it is often difficult to see.

Terminal hair is coarse and is found on the scalp, the underarms, and the pubic areas in women and men. Terminal hair also grows on the arms, legs, chest,

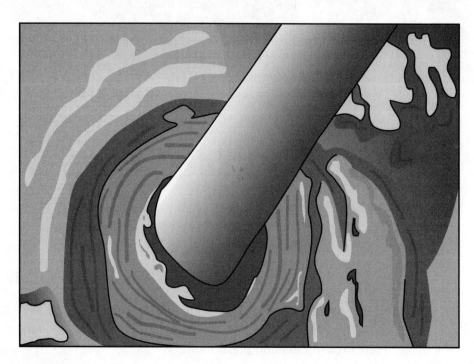

FIGURE 2-1 Microscopic view of hair follicle

back, and face of men. On average, a person whose scalp and hair are healthy will grow hair at a rate of half an inch per month.

Hair Growth

Hair growth is a genetic characteristic. Hair length, amount, color, texture, and pattern are determined at birth and are related to family traits. Cutting hair has no effect whatsoever on its growth. The average adult human scalp contains 100,000 to 350,000 hair follicles and the average person sheds 100 to 150 hairs per day. This hair loss by a healthy person is normal and is replaced with new hair without the lost hair ever being missed.

Hair grows below the skin in the hair bulb, which rests in the hair follicle (Figure 2-1). Here, hair is produced from the multiple growth of specialized cells that line the inner hair follicle at its root. This area is constantly fed by the blood supply from the hair papilla, which is an extension of the dermis. As the cells germinate in the hair bulb, they come together to form a solid structure.

Hair growth is not a continuous process. Hair follicles undergo three separate, alternating phases of existence—the anagen, the catagen, and the telogen. Growth occurs only in the anagen phase. The anagen phase is longer for scalp hair than for body hair. This phase also lasts longer in women than in men.

As growth slows, follicles begin to atrophy and hair separates from the follicle and falls out. This is the catagen or transitional phase. In the resting or telogen phase, the follicles are inactive and have shrunk to about half their normal size. After a relatively short rest period, they regenerate themselves and again begin producing hair. Hair growth cycles are staggered among the follicles. Not all of the follicles produce hair at the same time.

Each follicle follows its own cycle. At any given time, 85 percent of the follicles are in the anagen phase. Two percent are in the catagen phase and 13 percent in the telogen phase. In people with normally functioning hair follicles, the anagen phase can last up to five years, the catagen phase up to three weeks, and the telogen phase up to twelve weeks.

Some hair shedding is a normal part of the telogen phase. However, male pattern baldness is a genetic trait. The most common form is bitemporal hair loss and is shared equally by black and white men. Crown pattern baldness, which occurs at the scalp vertex is less common and occurs later in blacks. Because hair length and growth are determined at birth, products promoted to grow hair do not really grow new hair as much as they promote better hair care, which in turn, extends the growth cycle to its maximum length.

The scalp is an area of the skin and its structure is the same as skin anywhere else on the body. The scalp, however, is an area of high activity and is highly complex. Hair-producing cells in the follicles divide more rapidly than any other cells in the body except for those in the bone marrow. The scalp in black skin is usually drier because of the curved hair follicles, which prevent the oils from passing freely through them.

The scalp is often exposed to harmful depredations. Overly aggressive daily grooming of the hair is a major cause of scalp irritation. The idea of brushing the hair vigorously 100 strokes per day is a harmful myth that can easily lead to serious hair damage. Some products commonly used in the care of black hair can irritate the scalp and create dryness, too. No-lye relaxers can be especially drying to the scalp because of the longer processing time they require.

Dandruff is a condition caused by an accelerated turnover of skin cells on the scalp and consequent flaking off in clumps. Some medical conditions, certain hair-care products, and inherent scalp dryness can all cause dandruff.

Seborrheac dermatitis and psoriasis can be present on the scalp, just as they can be present on any other area of the skin. All of these conditions can be present in black skin. Contact dermatitis, the dryness, itching, flaking, and pustules, can be caused by hair care products such as relaxers and hot combs. Any of these conditions can lead to temporary or permanent hair loss.

BASIC HAIR STRUCTURE

Black hair and Caucasian hair consist of the same basic structural materials. Both are made from keratin, which is also a basic structural material of skin. Keratin, a protein derived from amino acids, is composed of organic compounds containing carbon, nitrogen, and hydrogen. Keratin also contains sulfur.

Cystine, the sulfur-containing amino acid from which keratin derives, is a major structural component of hair and the one on which relaxers and permanent waves work to alter the shape of the hair.

Black hair generally has a larger diameter and retains less water than white hair. The follicle in black hair is curved and produces hair that is twisted in a spiral. The cross-sectional shape of black hair tends to be flatter, more elliptical than round.

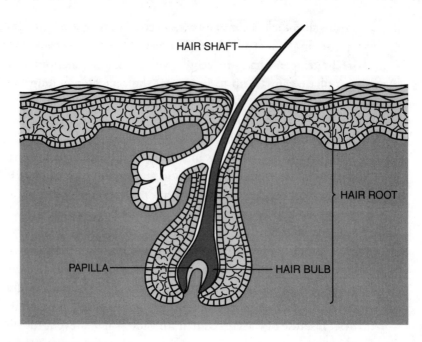

FIGURE 2-2 Hair structure

These characteristics—lower water content, curved follicles, and flatter hair shape—may account for the "kinky" hair common to most black people. These same characteristics may also account for difficulty in combining the hair, excessive breakage, and decreasing gloss.

Hair is divided into two basic parts: the shaft and the root (Figure 2-2). The shaft is the part that extends above the skin surface; the root is the part that is below the surface. The bulb is at the lower end of the root, covering the papilla, which nourishes it. Only the root actually grows. The root is living tissue. The shaft, on the other hand, is nonliving matter.

The three horny layers in the hair shaft are the cuticle, the cortex, and the medulla. The outer layer, the cuticle, is transparent. The middle layer, the cortex, contains the pigment that gives the hair its color. Together, these two layers give the hair its strength, flexibility, moisture absorbency, color, and shine. The innermost layer, the medulla, makes up the core of the hair shaft. Its exact functions are not well defined. The hair shaft has no nerve endings, thus, no sensations are felt through the hair, which is why it does not hurt to get a haircut.

The cuticles of black hair tend to be rougher than those in white hair. As a result, black hair cuticles reflect less light, giving a dull appearance to the hair. Because black hair cuticles are less absorbent to moisture, they react differently to chemicals than white hair, and therefore may require special moisturizers and chemical treatments that are longer or different. Black hair cuticles generally have larger melanin granules than those in white hair. This may be the reason black hair lightens in shorter time than white hair.

Black hair has a smaller cortex than white hair. This also affects chemical treatments. Timing is especially critical for chemical treatments on black hair, so these services should be performed only by someone highly trained in their use. Once the chemicals pass through the cuticle, they will work quickly on the smaller cortex and alter its structure faster. Black women have a special problem because of this. If the cortex is overprocessed, the hair will become weak and dull and will break off.

The smaller cortex in black hair leads also to a somewhat different sulfur structure and a lower lipid content. The sulfur bonds in black hair are slanted at sharp angles. The bonds are angled in the spiral hair follicle. This accounts for the curly nature of black hair.

The lower lipid content is evident in the inherent dryness common to black hair. Another possible cause of dry hair inherent in blacks is that as hair oils are produced by the sebaceous glands and secreted into the spiral hair follicles, the oils do not always get to the surface to moisturize the hair and scalp.

HAIR ANALYSIS

Just like the skin, the hair should be analyzed to determine its type and condition before performing any grooming service or chemical treatment. Hair type is described as straight, wavy or curly, or excessively curly. Each of these types has structural differences. Straight hair is round; wavy hair is oval; curly hair is flat. These are general guidelines, however, and not absolutes. The true variations in hair types are endless because of the possible genetic mix.

Black and Asian hair types are different from white hair types. These differences are described in terms of density, structure, content, and attainable length, all of which are critical factors in formulating hair care products and performing hair services.

Black hair tends to be shorter in length, with an elliptical, almost kidney-shaped form. It requires less force to remove from the scalp and has a higher amino acid content than either white or Asian hair types. Black hair has a greater density than white hair but a lower density than Asian hair. Black hair services commonly include exposing the hair to high temperatures, as in hot combing, and exposing it to harsh chemicals, as with relaxing, waving, and coloring. This can lead to hair dryness and breakage. In addition, combing black hair puts tremendous mechanical tension on the hair, causing even more dryness and breakage.

Asian hair is normally straight. It grows to greater lengths and has a higher density than either black or white hair. Asian hair requires a greater force than is required with either black or white hair to pull it from the scalp. It is round in shape and has a comparatively low amino acid content. Services for Asian hair are similar to those for white hair. Permanent wave and color treatments can leave Asian hair with a dull and rough appearance.

Hair *texture* is determined by the size of the individual strands. The diameter of the hair is based on the size of the cuticle and the cortex. Coarse hair tends to be larger in diameter than fine hair. This is probably because of the larger cuticle common to coarse and curly black hair.

Hair texture can be divided into seven categories, based on strand diameter: very fine, fine, medium fine, medium, medium coarse, coarse, and very coarse. However, any given strand can have a combination of these textures throughout its length.

Hair Condition

Hair condition is determined by a strand test. One aspect is its *porosity*, or ability to absorb moisture. The more porous the hair, the faster it will absorb moisture. Black hair is less porous than white hair; consequently, chemical treatments require longer times to work.

The second aspect determining hair condition is *elasticity*. Elasticity is the ability of the hair to bend and stretch without breaking off. Hair with good elasticity can tolerate chemical treatments better.

The third and final aspect of hair condition is *density*. Hair density is determined by the number of hairs per square inch. Thick hair will have more hairs per square inch than thin hair. Hair density is not related to hair texture. Fine hair can have a high density, just as coarse hair can have a low density.

Hair analysis is the first critical step in the proper care and treatment of the hair. It is important for the stylist and the consumer to realize that different types of hair can differ in response to chemical services.

HAIR CARE

Shampooing

Black hair tends to be naturally curly and somewhat dry and dull, and it breaks easily. Because frequent shampooing can further dry the hair and accelerate breakage, black hair generally should be shampooed less frequently (once or twice a week) than white hair. White hair, on the other hand, tends to be oily and requires frequent shampooing to prevent oil buildup and limp hair.

Once black hair is wet, it spontaneously starts to curl. This makes styling very difficult. Black hair is not cut while wet because it would be dramatically shorter after it dries. Also, black hair usually requires a special heating or chemical treatment to style (straighten) the hair. This is most commonly done in a salon. Black women tend to visit their salons at least two to three times a month.

Shampooing is designed to clean the scalp and hair. Because of its characteristics, serious consideration must be given to choosing a shampoo for black hair; the choice should be based on the hair type and condition. A person's hair history, home hair-care regimen, and personal preferences are also important.

Shampoos for black hair most often will need to contain mild detergent cleaners and moderate to heavy conditioners, and have a balanced pH.

Most medicated or dandruff-control shampoos contain ingredients such as tar derivatives, sulfur, selenium sulfide, zinc pyrithione, and salicylic acid. They are formulated to work on the scalp to remove dead skin cells and to slow down cell turnover rate. They can be extremely drying to the hair and scalp. Therefore, these shampoos are seldom effective on black hair, nor are they recommended because they can further dry black hair and scalp.

To shampoo properly, first wet the hair thoroughly with warm water, then pour a small amount (about the size of a silver dollar) of shampoo into the palm of the hand. Gently massage the shampoo into the scalp starting at the sides of the head near the ears. Gently massage in a back and forth motion from the front hairline to the nape of the neck. Rinse the shampoo from the hair thoroughly with lots of warm water. Repeat the process if necessary. Always make sure to rinse the hair until it is completely free of residual shampoo.

Hair Conditioners

After shampooing, hair has a positive charge, which repels each strand and prevents the hair from lying down, making it more difficult to manage. Hair conditioners are designed to provide moisture, shine, and manageability to hair. They accomplish this by giving the cuticle a neutral charge, thus restoring it to a smooth state and decreasing the ability of the hair to stick together. When it has a neutral charge, black hair becomes easier to comb and brush.

Conditioners also normalize cuticles by alleviating defects in the cuticles to give hair a shine and decrease tangling. Normalized cuticles reflect light more, giving hair a shine. Because strands do not stick together, tangling is decreased and overall manageability is increased. Black hair requires the applications of conditioners after each shampooing.

Three types of conditioners are used with black hair: instant, deep penetrating, and hot oil. *Instant conditioners* are the products used commonly after shampooing in the home and in the salon. They require no mixing and are used right from the bottle. These conditioners are available in various formulations based on hair type and condition. Conditioners formulated with quaternary ammonium compounds work best with black hair. They are excellent for moisturizing the hair, neutralizing the charge on hair to prevent tangling, and providing good shine after smoothing cuticles.

Deep penetrating conditioners are designed for use on dry and damaged hair. They are a concentrated form of instant conditioners and are usually found in a cream form that requires activation by the application of heat, as with a hair dryer or a warm towel. The heat is usually applied for twenty to thirty minutes to allow the hair shaft to swell, increasing porosity and absorption of conditioners that seal and repair damaged cuticles.

Hot oil conditioners are designed to treat extra dry and damaged hair. This treatment is somewhat of a misnomer in that the oils only coat the hair. The actual work is done by proteins and polymers. Hot oil treatments require heating the oil and applying it to the hair, then covering the hair with a plastic cap for the recommended period of time. The treatment provides a shine to the hair and helps repair damaged cuticles.

The hair shaft consists of dead keratin, just like the stratum corneum layer of the skin. The only conditioning treatment that will work is one that coats the hair shaft. Proper conditioning of black hair makes it more manageable, easier to comb and brush; it gives hair a shine and makes it less likely to break. Because the ends are the oldest part of the hair as well as its driest part, apply the conditioners specifically to the end tips and comb thoroughly to provide even distribution of conditioner to the entire hair shaft from the top of the scalp to the end of each hair. Leave the conditioner on for the entire time stated in the manufacturer's instructions.

HAIRCOLORING

Hair, as well as skin, can change its color with age. Gray hair usually appears in whites in their thirties and in blacks in their forties. Coloring the hair can prolong a youthful appearance as well as give the hair more depth, volume, silkiness, and contrast. Haircoloring can be used for more than covering gray and restoring the hair's natural color, however. It can also be used to change the hair's natural color. This requires somewhat more care with black hair than with white hair. The haircolor chosen should complement the person's natural skin tones and eye coloration.

Natural hair color is determined by melanin granules in the cuticle and cortex of the hair strand. The hair's natural color can be changed by artificial means, either by adding color to the natural pigment or by lightening the natural pigment. When lightened, hair goes through seven levels of color change: black, brown, red, red-gold, gold, yellow, and pale yellow.

The natural color of black hair ranges from dark brown with reddish overtones to jet black. Covering gray and restoring hair's natural color can be accomplished with single-process coloring or, in some cases, with rinses. Making the hair darker than its natural color can also be accomplished with single-process coloring. However, making the hair color significantly lighter than its natural color will almost always require a double-process coloring in which the hair is first stripped of its natural color and then the new tint is applied.

For the most part, the same products and haircoloring techniques used on white hair can be used on black hair, with allowances for time and application procedures for the increased coarseness and porosity of black hair. Coloring black hair is an area that should only be done by trained professionals who are experienced in coloring black hair. Relaxed hair should not be colored permanently. The stress of so much chemical treatment will almost assuredly cause hair breakage and damage. Rinses, however, may be used. As with any chemical service, a patch test and hair analysis should be completed before hair is colored.

There are four categories of artificial haircoloring: gradual, temporary, semi-permanent, and permanent.

Gradual Haircoloring

Gradual haircoloring is achieved by the daily application of a product containing a metallic dye that gradually darkens the hair over a two- to three-week time span. Most of these products are over-the-counter items sold at retail outlets. The metallic dyes most often used are compounds of lead and silver. Over time, these products can cause the hair to appear dull. They may also weaken the hair and lead to hair breakage. The products are safe to the hair, however, because they do not penetrate the cuticle. They only coat the hair shaft.

Previous use of metallic dye products can alter the results of any chemical service. It is important to let your stylist know whether or not you have used these products before beginning any other type of chemical service.

Temporary Haircoloring

Temporary haircoloring lasts from shampoo to shampoo and is accomplished with rinses that must be reapplied frequently. The rinses, which are acid-based dyes, only improve the existing color. Like the metallic dyes, rinses coat the cuticle without penetrating into the hair shaft. As a result, they are not likely to damage the hair.

When using a rinse to add color to the cuticle of black hair, the color service should be planned to coincide with a relaxer service. This will enhance and prolong the hair color.

Semipermanent Haircoloring

As the name of the category implies, semipermanent haircoloring lasts longer than shampoo to shampoo but does not permanently change the hair color. Hair colored by this method will hold color through four to six shampoo cycles.

Semipermanent haircoloring is achieved with synthetic or natural dyes that produce a tone-on-tone color change. They do not produce dramatic color changes. Synthetic dyes are coal tar derivatives that must be approved by the Food and Drug Administration for cosmetic use.

Natural dyes are derived from vegetable matter and are the oldest type of haircolorants known. The most common natural dye is henna, which comes from the henna plant. The form most used today is compound henna, in which metallic dyes are added to the henna to give a wider range of colors. Compound henna is safer to use than natural henna, which can cause dryness, stiffness, and hair breakage. Natural henna does have a very low allergic profile, however.

Semipermanent haircolorants, whether natural or synthetic, cannot lighten darker hair. They can only make hair darker. They can darken lighter hair up to three shades. These products penetrate the cuticle and reach the cortex, although they do this without using ammonia and hydrogen peroxide. Body temperature and dryer heat decrease reaction time for the products to work and increase the level of penetration of the dye to the cortex.

Permanent Haircoloring

Permanent haircoloring changes the chemical structure of the hair and, as a result, lasts until the hair grows out enough to require a touch-up. This could be anywhere from four to six weeks after the initial coloring takes place. The natural color of the hair can be lightened or darkened, depending on the new color desired.

Permanent haircoloring is the most common type of hair coloring in current use. Formulations are available for home use as well as for professional salon use. The chemistry is basically the same regardless of the formulation, although those products designed for professional salon use are typically stronger and allow more dramatic changes in hair color.

In general, permanent haircoloring products consist of hydrogen peroxide, ammonia, and a colorant. The formulation works by penetrating the hair shaft into the cortex. To lighten the hair and prepare it to accept the colorant, the melanin granules that give the hair its natural color have to be destroyed by a chemical reaction known as oxidation. Hydrogen peroxide is the oxidizing agent that accomplishes this step. The ammonia is an activating agent for the peroxide. The colorant provides the color.

A number of different colorants are used for permanent haircoloring. The most commonly used are aniline derivative tints, which have some oxidizing action of their own. These colorants are known to cause allergic reactions or contact dermatitis in a certain percentage of the population. When using any of these products, it is necessary to conduct a patch test first.

To conduct a patch test, mix a small amount of the product as it would be used normally, then apply a small amount of it to the back of the ear area and leave on for twenty-four hours. If the test is negative, that is, there is no reaction, the product may be used. If the test is positive, that is, there is redness, swelling, itching, blistering, or pain, the product should not be used.

Hair damage is quite common with permanent haircoloring. The hair can become dull and lifeless as well as discolored, and it can weaken and break. Special conditioning steps may be prudent to maintain the health of the hair. Hair relaxing or permanent wave treatments should not be given within ten days of coloring the hair and should be conducted only by a trained and experienced professional.

Permanent haircoloring treatments can be either single process or double process. Both processes can lighten or darken the hair color. Most home coloring formulations are single process. Professional treatments can use either.

In single-process coloring, the colorant is mixed with the peroxide. The mixture is applied as a single step. The peroxide lifts the color and prepares the cortex for the colorant. The colorant finishes the work.

In double-process coloring, two steps are used. First, hydrogen peroxide is used to remove the existing color. Second, the colorant is used to provide the new color. The double-process treatment results in the most dramatic color changes.

Because of its thicker cuticle, virgin black hair has a low porosity and is more resistant to haircoloring than Caucasian hair. However, the various chemical treatments that black hair requires can increase the porosity, making black hair more receptive to coloring. The cortex in black hair is thinner than in Caucasian hair. As a result, once the color formulation gets past the cuticle, the time required to color the hair is reduced.

Lightening black hair requires a higher concentration of hydrogen peroxide than is needed to lighten Caucasian hair. Whereas twenty volume hydrogen peroxide is normal for use on Caucasian hair, for black hair, the concentration may reach twenty-five to thirty volume. Black hair should never be lightened beyond the red-gold level because that will almost always cause damage. Black hair that has been chemically treated with perms or relaxers should not be lightened.

BRAIDING AND HAIR WEAVING

Braiding and hair weaving are currently popular fashions, particularly among black women. Both are similar, in that they are made by interweaving strands of hair. Braiding, however, is done solely with the person's natural hair. Hair weaving, on the other hand, uses human hair that has been matched to the person's natural hair for color and texture. This supplemental hair, as it were, is woven into braids intertwined with the natural hair.

These styles are accomplished by mechanical actions, with no chemicals used, so there is no concern about chemical irritation. However, the tight braids currently in vogue can lead to some hair damage. It takes a considerable amount of time—sometimes as long as eight hours—to have such braiding or weaving done. Once done, the braids are kept in for weeks. With very tight braids, it is difficult to properly clean the scalp and hair because water and shampoos cannot penetrate into the braids. This can create problems with skin irritation and inflection. To overcome this, some women wash their braided hair with water pics designed for dental use.

In addition, tight braiding can cause breakage and hair loss due to a condition known as traction alopeceia, in which the hair is almost literally pulled out of its roots.

HAIR LOSS

Hair loss is defined as the obvious loss of large amounts of scalp hair or body hair or as the loss of the quality of scalp hair, for example, diminishment of diameter, length, and density.

Hair loss can be caused by a number of conditions, some of which can affect only the hair, or only the scalp, or a combination of both. Some common causes of hair loss include poor diet, rapid weight loss, drugs, family history (i.e., genetic predisposition), recent illnesses, improper hair care, aging, and hormone imbalances. Hair can also be lost in a period starting two to three months after pregnancy and can last for up to nine months. Hair loss as a result of excessive breakage is usually caused by improper hair care.

Androgenic Alopeceia

The most common form of hair loss in women and men is androgenic alopeceia. Thirty percent of Caucasian women are affected with this condition before the onset of menopause. Androgenic alopeceia is sometimes reversible with medical treatment, but the results of treatment are unpredictable. Results depend on individual sensitivity to medical treatment. This form of alopeceia is believed to be caused by higher-than-normal levels of circulating androgens that stimulate genetically sensitive hair follicles and shorten the anagen phase of the hair growth cycle. At the same time, there is an increased shedding of hair from follicles in the telogen phase.

Pattern Baldness

Male pattern baldness occurs in the frontotemporal regions and at the vertex. Female pattern baldness is more diffuse although hair is not usually lost on the frontal hairline. Either pattern can be seen in women of any age.

Traumatic Alopeceia

Traumatic alopeceia is common in blacks and is caused by chemical and mechanical abuse of the hair and scalp. Chemical treatments can cause extreme breakage of the hair and lead to this type of alopeceia. Tightly braiding the hair can also cause severe irritation to the scalp, which releases the hair from the follicle and causes the condition. Traumatic alopeceia is usually reversible. The condition is best treated with better hair care.

Alopeceia Areata

Alopeceia areata is sometimes a reversible form of hair loss that features well-circumscribed, nonscarring patches of baldness. This is a common condition among almost all age groups beyond the teen years. There is a considerable variation in the rate and pattern of hair loss and regrowth. Most sufferers of this condition are in good general health, although a number of diseases have also been associated with the onset of alopeceia areata. These include asthma, atopic dermatitis, diabetes, thyroid disease, ulcerative colitis, and vitiligo.

Ten percent of people with alopeceia areata also undergo changes in the nails. These changes include pitting, longitudinal ridging, thickening, brittleness, and onchylysis. Twenty-five percent of people have a family history of the condition.

In 90 percent of the cases, the condition follows a pattern in which there is patchy hair loss for a three- to six-month period. This is followed by a three- to six-month period of stability, after which there is a three- to six-month period of gradual regrowth. Recurrence of the condition is common, although complete permanent hair loss is rare.

There is no consistent effective treatment for alopeceia areata. The course of treatment is variable between regrowth and remission stages. Currently available treatments include topical and injectable steroids, minoxidil, psoralen plus ultra-violet A (PUVA), and perhaps most important, psychological support from family and friends.

Telogen Effluvium

Telogen effluvium is an abrupt form of hair loss in which half or less of the scalp hair is lost because of a severe assault on the body's metabolism. The stimulus for the condition causes a large number of anagen hairs to convert to telogen hairs with subsequent shedding. The condition normally appears one to four months after the metabolic event. Some metabolic assaults that can lead to telogen effluvium include childbirth, chronic illness, rapid weight change, high fever, hypothyroidism, psychological stress, surgery, and systemic infection. No treatment is necessary for this condition because it is inherently self-limiting. Hair regrowth is almost always complete within six months to a year.

Anagen Effluvium

Anagen effluvium is also associated with metabolic assault. In this condition, there is a rapid and incomplete conversion of anagen hair to telogen hair leading to the diffuse shedding of 85 percent to 90 percent of the scalp hair. This condition is similar to telogen effluvium but occurs to a greater degree. Regrowth is common when the underlying metabolic condition is corrected.

Drug-Induced Alopeceia

In drug-induced alopeceia, drugs taken or chemicals used increase the number of hairs in the telogen phase, which leads to telogen effluvium. It can also be caused when the drugs or chemicals produce a dermatologic condition that features alopeceia as a symptom. A wide variety of drugs can cause drug-induced alopeceia, including amphetamines, haloperidol, heparin, indomethacin, isotretinoin, lithium, propranol, and many others. Treatment for the condition consists of controlling or eliminating the offending drug.

Scarring Alopeceia

In scarring alopeceia, the capacity of the follicle to function is lost because of trauma or disease. The condition is irreversible. The most common disease that causes scarring alopeceia is discoid lupus erythematosus (DLE). DLE lesions can be seen in people with systemic disease involvement, although they are commonly seen alone as well. In black women, the lesions are most common in areas of the skin exposed to the sun.

The scarring shows as a hypopigmented, atrophic plaque with teleangectasia on the face, neck, ears, and scalp. UV light makes the lesions worse, so sun protection is mandatory. The cause of DLE is unknown. Treatment is more effective on early lesions. The condition is treated with anti-inflammatory steroids.

Hair loss is a common complaint. See your physician for diagnosis and treatment. These are, for the most part, medical conditions that require the services of a trained, licensed physician.

HAIR-LOSS SOLUTIONS FOR WOMEN

Women who have thinning hair have many of the same options as men. Cuts that conceal the thinning area, body perms, and creative styling techniques all come into play. Younger women often favor hair integration systems. (They work for men, too.) These light pieces have an open mesh base and look somewhat like hairnets with large open areas. Integration systems, which come premade—or can be custom ordered or handmade—have hair attached to the base. The natural hair is pulled through the venting and is integrated with the hair from the integration piece. They are excellent for a woman who has allover thinning and can also be designed for people who have specific pattern balding. Because integration systems can be created with bangs and cut so the hair falls forward, they are also ideal for the person who has a fragile hairline or even severe hairline breakage. The hairline is concealed and allowed to restore itself, if damage is not permanent.

Hair Integration Systems

Custom integration systems have webbing that is usually crocheted. Hair of any length, texture, curl configuration, or density can be added along the lines of the base or webbing. This allows you to add more hair wherever it is needed and even make adjustments for changes in texture within the hair.

Lois Christie of Christie & Co. in Bayside, New York, specializes in custom-made integration systems. According to her, systems can be created for any hair type. Hair knows no nationality; understanding the varieties of hair texture is essential for creating custom integration systems. Even someone who has 75 percent hair loss can wear an integration system; only large bald areas are a contraindication for using one.

Christie recommends taking at least an hour for a consultation to discuss cost, the procedure, realistic expectations, and maintenance. Systems average between 750 and 1500 dollars and generally must be replaced twice a year.

Once you understand the system, a mold is created, just as it is for a hairpiece. The stylist will secure plastic wrap over your head with a band and mark the areas of hair loss with clear tape and marker, noting where the perimeter of the base will end, where more density is desired, and so forth. This mold is sent to the manufacturer along with a sample of hair and notes on its texture, color, curl configuration, and percentage of gray. A mesh base with a blend of synthetic and human hair is created.

Attachment methods for integration systems are similar to those available for hairpieces. They can be sewn onto tracks, as long as you have enough natural hair to create the tracks, or they can be bonded to the natural hair. This method lasts four to six weeks. They can also be attached with spring clips or locking combs if you want to remove the piece at night.

When the system arrives, it generally has more hair than desired so it can be cut and tapered. It is rare that more hair will be added.

Christie relates care of the system to care of your finest silk blouse. Gentle shampooing should be performed with a mild cleanser. Overuse of conditioners should be avoided or slippage might occur. Condition the ends of the hair only and avoid oil or lanolin-based conditioners. Application of light gels and minimal use of hairspray will extend the life of the system; mousses tend to get gummy on the synthetic hair. If you have relaxed hair, avoid overuse of oil-based products and styling creams, because these could also cause slippage in the tracking. The system should be adjusted in the salon every four to six weeks, depending on the rate of hair growth. At that time, chemical touch-ups can be performed. No matter how delicately the hair is handled, it will not last a lifetime; plan on ordering a new system twice a year.

Hair Additions for Specific Hair-Loss Patterns

Hair additions provide another excellent option for women and men. Wefts can be added where they are needed; even if there is a completely bald patch on the head, the thread weaving technique can be used to extend the track across an area where there is no hair. For men, wefts are cut short and selected to match the natural hair texture.

Hair Additions for Hair That Is Thinning All Over

If the natural hair has thinned all over and the hairline has begun to recede, all the remaining hair on the head can be incorporated into braids, to which wefts will be attached. In this technique, very wide partings are used to incorporate enough hair to create a braid. (The width depends on how thin the hair is.) The technique is not recommended if there is hairline breakage. It is ideal for fine or mature hair, but may not be the best solution if actual bald patches exist.

Each parting will be about a quarter-inch to a half-inch wide, depending on how much hair you have to work with. Braids are created around the entire circumference of the head, working from the hairline to the crown in progressively smaller circles. Then wefts are attached. A layered cut that includes bangs conceals all the tracks. Human hair wefts may work best with this technique, because the layers can easily be iron curled or blow dried for added volume.

Hair Addition Solutions for Hairline Breakage

If you have breakage at the hairline, it is often because of improperly applied chemicals. Repeated overlapping of relaxers or use of too harsh chemicals for your hair type take their toll over time. In addition, permed and bleached hair often suffers from breakage, particularly at the fragile hairline.

After a thorough hair analysis and scalp examination, if your scalp is healthy and most of the hair is in good condition, you have several options to conceal damage, restore healthy hair, and give the hair a break from chemicals.

An integration system with extra density at the front can be used to create bangs that conceal the area with most breakage. Another option that allows you to have braids conceals the hairline completely and more permanently. One approach uses bangs; the other uses asymmetrical braids that are positioned to fall over the hairline. In both techniques, individual braids are created and synthetic hair, which can be sealed at the ends, is used.

CHAPTER 3

Products for Black Skin and Hair Care

Good products are essential to good skin care. Although skin care treatments can be given without the aid of machinery, they are virtually impossible to give without using some type of product formulated for some aspect of skin care.

For the most part, skin care products are not ethnic specific, that is, most products on the market can be used on black skin as well as white skin. However, some products have been specially formulated for use on black skin. These include products such as skin toners, which are used to lighten skin and even out coloration.

Many excellent skin care products are on the market, as well as many that are not so good. The esthetician or the consumer has to make intelligent choices from a sometimes dazzling array of materials and has to cut through the clutter and hype of advertising claims.

It is important to understand the products used in skin care. It is necessary to know what is in those products, why those things are there, and what effect they have. It is also necessary to know what products are available, and under what situations they are of most use.

REVIEW OF CHEMISTRY

All life on earth depends on chemistry. Without chemicals and chemical processes, there would be no existence at all. Chemistry can be loosely divided into two branches: inorganic and organic. *Organic chemistry* is concerned with compounds that contain carbon, the essential component for all living things. *Inorganic chemistry* is concerned with compounds that do not contain carbon, essentially all nonliving things. The boundaries are rather loose, though. Water (H_2O) is an inorganic compound as is air, which is a compound of oxygen, nitrogen, and small amounts of other gases. Gasoline, a hydrocarbon, is an organic compound, as is acetone. Hydrocarbons, that is, substances that contain carbon and hydrogen, are among the most important organic compounds. Skin care products fall into both categories. Some are organic compounds and some are inorganic compounds.

In addition, *biochemistry* is a subbranch of organic chemistry and deals with the chemical processes in living organisms. Amino acids, proteins, carbohydrates, and vitamins are examples of biochemicals.

Chemistry, regardless of branch, is the study of matter, the fundamental materials of the world, and its three states: solids, the ground we walk on; liquid, the water we drink; and gas, the air we breathe. Everything consists of one of these three forms of matter.

Matter consists of *elements,* which can exist singly or together in mixtures and compounds. There are 105 elements known although relatively few exist in great abundance. The human body, for example, consists primarily of three: carbon, oxygen, and hydrogen. There are other elements in the body, but they occur in small amounts. Table 3-1 lists the elements.

Mixtures consist of two or more elements intermingled physically but not chemically. Each element keeps its own characteristics. Take for example, salt and pepper. If they are mixed together, the result is a salt and pepper mixture that could be separated if someone wanted to get a pair of tweezers and a magnifying glass and take the time to do it. But the salt is still salt and the pepper is still pepper. *Compounds,* on the other hand, consist of two or more elements that combine chemically to form a different substance. The initial elements cannot be separated physically. Water is a good example. Water consists of two atoms of hydrogen (H) and one atom of oxygen (O)—two gases that combine to form the liquid compound, water (H_2O). The two elements have become something else. The hydrogen and the oxygen have both lost their original identities. Salt (NaCl) is a compound consisting of one atom of sodium (Na) and one atom of chlorine (Cl).

Elements differ from one another in their atomic structure. Each one consists of *atoms,* which are the smallest unit of the element that can combine with other elements. Atoms consist of subatomic particles: *protons* and *neutrons* in the core or nucleus of the atom, and *electrons* in orbit around the nucleus. The number of protons determines the characteristics of the element, thus its identity.

Molecules are combinations of atoms bound tightly together. The atoms can be alike or different. One molecule of oxygen, for example, consists of two atoms of oxygen. One molecule of water consists of one atom of oxygen and two atoms of hydrogen.

This information is fine in theory, but why is it important? It is important because it explains how and why the products used in skin care work. You will work with solid, liquid, and gaseous products. Some of the products will be mixtures; some will be compounds. The size of the molecules of the product determines whether or not it will penetrate into the skin.

When different substances are mixed, a chemical reaction occurs. It is this reaction that creates the new substance, called the product. This product can be another chemical substance, or it can be energy in the form of heat, as in the digestion process, or electricity, as in a car battery. Estheticians are most concerned with oxidation-reduction reactions and neutralization reactions. Most biologic processes are examples of oxidation-reduction reactions. Neutralization reactions do just what they imply. They neutralize the actions of acids and bases.

Acids and *bases* are among the most important chemicals the esthetician works with. Many of the products used in skin care have either acidic or basic properties. Acids have a sour taste and turn litmus paper red. Bases, or alkalies, have a bitter taste and a slippery feel and turn litmus paper blue. Acids and bases can also be classified as either organic or inorganic. Hydrochloric acid (HCl), secreted by the

TABLE 3-1	Elements		

NAME	SYMBOL	ATOMIC NUMBER	ATOMIC WEIGHT
Actinium*	Ac	89	227
Aluminum	Al	13	27
Americum*	Am	95	243
Antimony	Sb	51	121.8
Argon	Ar	18	39.9
Arsenic	As	33	74.9
Astatine*	At	85	210
Barium	Ba	56	137.3
Berkelium*	Bk	97	247
Beryllium	Be	4	9
Bismuth	Bi	83	209
Boron	B	5	10.8
Bromine	Br	35	79.9
Cadmium	Cd	48	112.4
Calcium*	Ca	20	40.1
Californium*	Cf	98	249
Carbon	C	6	12
Cerium	Ce	58	140.1
Cesium	Cs	55	132.9
Chlorine**	Cl	17	35.5
Chromium**	Cr	24	52
Cobalt**	Co	27	58.9
Copper**	Cu	29	63.5
Curium*	Cm	96	247
Dysprosium	Dy	66	162.5
Einsteinium*	Es	99	254
Erbium	Er	68	167.3
Europium	Eu	63	152
Fermium*	Fm	100	253
Fluorine**	F	9	19
Francium*	Fr	87	223
Gadolinium	Gd	64	157.3
Gallium	Ga	31	69.7
Germanium	Ge	32	72.6
Gold	Au	79	197
Hafnium	Hf	72	178.5
Haxxxdum*	Ha	105	260
Helium	He	2	4
Holmium	Ho	67	165
Hydrogen	H	1	1
Indium	In	49	114.8
Iodine**	I	53	126.9
Iridium	Ir	77	192.2
Iron**	Fe	26	55.9
Krypton	Kr	36	83.8
Lanthanum	La	57	138.9
Lawrencium*	Lw	103	257
Lead	Pb	82	207.2
Lithium	Li	3	7
Lutetium	Lu	71	175
Magnesium**	Mg	12	24.3
Manganese**	Mn	25	54.9
Mendelevium*	Md	101	256
Mercury	Hg	80	200.6
Molybdenum*	Mo	42	95.9
Neodymium	Nd	60	144.2
Neon	Ne	10	20.2
Neptunium*	Np	93	237
Nickel	Ni	28	58.7
Niobium	Nb	41	92.9
Nitrogen	N	7	14
Nobelium*	No	102	253
Osmium	Os	76	190.2
Oxygen	O	8	16
Palladium	Pd	46	106.4
Phosphorus**	P	15	31
Platinum	Pt	78	195.1
Plutonium*	Pu	94	242
Polonium*	Po	84	210
Potassium**	K	19	39.1
Praseodymium	Pr	59	140.9
Promethium*	Pm	61	147
Protactinium*	Pa	91	231
Radium*	Ra	88	226
Radon*	Rn	*6	222
Rhenium	Re	75	186.2
Rhodium	Rh	45	102.9
Rubidium	Rb	37	85.5

(continued)

TABLE 3-1		Elements—continued						

NAME	SYMBOL	ATOMIC NUMBER	ATOMIC WEIGHT	NAME	SYMBOL	ATOMIC NUMBER	ATOMIC WEIGHT
Ruthenium	Ru	44	101.1	Thallium	Tl	81	204.4
Rutherfordium*	Rf	104	257	Thorium	Th	90	232
Samarium	Sm	62	150.4	Thulium	Tm	69	168.9
Scandium	Sc	21	45	Tin	Sn	50	118.7
Selenium**	Se	34	79	Titanium	Ti	22	47.9
Silicon	Si	14	28.1	Tungsten	W	74	183.9
Silver	Ag	47	107.9	Uranium*	U	92	238
Sodium**	Na	11	23	Vanadium*	V	23	50.9
Strontium*	Sr	38	87.6	Xenon	Xe	54	131.3
Sulfur**	S	16	32	Ytterbium	Yb	70	173
Tantalum	Ta	73	180.9	Yttrium	Y	39	89
Technetium*	Tc	43	99	Zinc**	Zn	30	65.4
Tellurium	Te	52	127.6	Zirconium	Zr	40	91.2
Terbium	Tb	65	158.9				

*Radioactive elements

**Elements important to nutrition

stomach in the process of digestion, and sulfuric acid (H_2SO_4), found in car batteries, are inorganic acids. Phenol (HOC_6H_5), used in chemical skin peels, as well as the alpha-hydroxy acids, are organic acids. Caustic soda (NaOH) and ammonia (NH_3) are inorganic bases. Nicotine ($C_{10}H_{14}N_2$) is an organic base.

Although it is possible to tell whether a substance is acidic or alkaline with an indicator like litmus paper, that test does not tell how acidic or alkaline the substance is. The quantitative measure of acidity or alkalinity is pH. Simply speaking, pH is a logarithmic scale that measures the degree of acidity or alkalinity. The scale is measured from 0 to 14. From 0 to 7 is acidic; 7 is neutral; and from 7 to 14 is alkaline. But remember that this is a logarithmic scale, not linear, so 6 is 100% or twice as acid as 7; 5 is twice as acid as 6, and so on. The same ratio holds true in the other direction. Table 3-2 illustrates pH.

A few notable points here. Pure water is neutral. Normal skin has a pH of about 5.5. Extremely dry skin has a pH of about 3. Both are acidic. Extremely oily skin, on the other hand, has a pH of 9, meaning it is alkaline. This is a great concept. All that is necessary to determine skin type is to measure the pH. Unfortunately, it is not that simple. pH is hard to measure accurately without very expensive and highly technical laboratory equipment. The concept is important nonetheless, because many of the products used rely on their acidity or alkalinity, measured by pH, to do their work.

Solutions are important, particularly liquid solutions. A *solution* is a homogeneous compound, that is, the molecules of the components are mingled uniformly. Although most of the solutions estheticians work with are liquid, a

TABLE 3-2	pH Chart

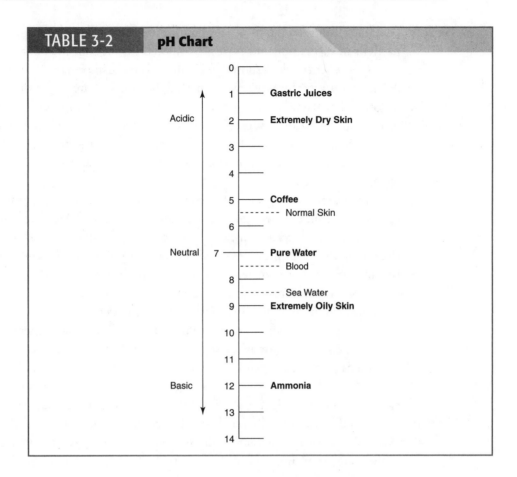

	0
Acidic	1 — **Gastric Juices**
	2 — **Extremely Dry Skin**
	3
	4
	5 — **Coffee**
	------ Normal Skin
	6
Neutral	7 — **Pure Water**
	------ Blood
	8
	------ Sea Water
	9 — **Extremely Oily Skin**
	10
	11
Basic	12 — **Ammonia**
	13
	14

solution can also be a gas, as in the air we breathe, or a solid, as in a metal alloy. Solutions consist of a *solute,* the substance being dissolved, and a *solvent,* the substance that dissolves the solute. Products use many different solvents, including alcohols, acids, and oils, but the most commonly used solvent in skin care products is water.

When it comes to solvents, attention centers on VOCs—volatile organic compounds from petroleum-based solvents, and their release into the atmosphere. They give the smell to products like nail polish removers. The Environmental Protection Agency (EPA) has virtually banned VOCs from the marketplace. Although their focus has been on industry, they may start monitoring businesses like beauty salons as well. Many manufacturers are looking at alternative solvents that will not release VOCs into the air.

When two liquids mix readily, they are said to be *miscible.* When they do not, they are said to be *immiscible.* Oils are not soluble in water; that is, oil and water do not mix. So when you have a product made with an oily component and a watery component, the manufacturer has to use a substance to keep the two phases from separating. That substance is called an *emulsifier.*

Remember the earlier discussion about the difference between compounds and mixtures. Solutions are compounds. In a liquid product when the molecules of the components do not intermingle but stay separate, the product is a heterogeneous mixture. When the particles are relatively large, the product is called a *suspension.* When they are relatively small, it is called a *colloid.* When a suspension or colloidal mixture sits on the shelf, the particles tend to settle to the bottom of the container. To overcome this, the manufacturer uses a dispersing agent to keep the particles in suspension and evenly distributed throughout the mixture.

Water is a marvelous substance. Only air is more important to human existence. A human can exist for weeks without food, but will die after being deprived of water for only a few days. Water is important to the body. It is important to the manufacture of most skin care products because it is the most commonly used solvent.

Water is not only a product component; it can be the product. When a vaporizer is used, the steam is a product. When you rinse cleanser from your face, the water is a product.

Pure water, that is, water that contains nothing but the proper mix of hydrogen and oxygen, has a pH of 7 and is absolutely neutral. However, the only time water is pure is when it is distilled or deionized. Natural water, as it comes out of the ground, is never pure. It contains dissolved minerals. The content and quantity of these minerals depend on the area the water comes from. In addition, municipal water is treated and contains chemicals such as chlorine and fluorine. Sea water has more minerals yet and is discussed later.

Calcium and magnesium are the most commonly found minerals dissolved in water. When water contains these minerals, it is known as hard water. Hard water keeps suds from forming in soap, causes rings around bathtubs, and leaves mineral deposits around heating elements. This is the reason the manufacturer of the vaporizer recommends the use of distilled water to generate the steam.

Manufacturers usually use distilled or deionized water to make their products. Water should be checked for hardness. Hardness is measured in grains per gallon. If the water measures more than about 16 grains per gallon, consider putting a water softener in the system. It will probably pay for itself in no time.

A water softener uses a deionization process that is more limited than the process used by manufacturers. In a water softener, the water passes over ion exchange beads that swap the metal mineral ions for sodium ions. The machines are regenerated with salt. At the same time, a filter should be installed to remove impurities such as iron, which is responsible for the red streaks sometimes found in laundry or in the toilet bowl.

PRODUCTS

The number of products available to the beauty industry is staggering. There are literally thousands of chemical products of various types, all competing for the buyer's attention.

Product choice starts with a close look at what is available. First, products can be grouped according to categories, that is, what they are used for—facial masks, toners, nail polish removers, permanent wave lotions, and so on. Within many product categories are subcategories, such as cleansers for oily skin, shampoos for dry hair, or those formulated to meet different ethnic needs.

The major factor in product proliferation is competition. With rare exception, every type of product is made by more than one manufacturer, with the result that there may be thirty different cleansers to choose from, or eighty-six different shampoos, or twenty-seven different moisturizers. Many of these products will be virtually identical except for the name on the package and the claims made by the manufacturer. How does one decide which to use?

It is not easy! But there is a logical way to approach the problem and a few very simple rules to keep in mind. First, consider what the product does. Each product has a purpose— a reason for being. This is expressed in its category. So the first thing to decide is what do you want the product to do? Next, what is its function? If the product does not accomplish something, it is useless, no matter how expensive it is, no matter how attractively it is packaged, no matter how much it has been promoted.

Product Categories

Skin care products can be separated by category. These are the categories most likely to be used every day.

- Cleansers rid the skin of dirt and other impurities, such as dead cells, makeup, and excess sebum. An effective cleanser cleans both the surface of the skin and the pores. It cleans thoroughly, without drying the skin excessively or stripping it of its protective oils. It rinses off the skin easily.

- Toners, fresheners, and astringents complete the cleaning process by removing cleanser residue and helping restore the acid mantle. They also refresh the skin. Toners are used on dry skin and do not contain alcohol or other drying ingredients. Fresheners are used on normal skin. Astringents are designed for use on oily skin and generally contain alcohol to help dissolve excess oil.

- Moisturizers and night creams prevent moisture loss from the skin and keep it moist. They also help protect the skin from the environment. They soften the skin and slow the effects of aging by keeping the skin moist. Moisturizers are designed primarily for daytime use. They deposit a thin film of water, oil, and emollient on the surface of the skin but do not penetrate the skin. The barrier formed by the moisturizer film holds the moisture in the skin.

- Night creams are similar to moisturizers. They also help retard moisture loss but also contain ingredients that help repair skin damage. These products, meant to be used at night while the body is resting, do penetrate to a limited degree. Their ingredients help restore cellular function and soothe and nourish the skin. Moisturizers can be covered with makeup, but night creams should be left uncovered.

- Eye and throat creams are products designed to provide nutrients and lubrication to those areas around the eyes and on the neck that have little natural oil of their own. These products are most useful with dry, aging skin.

- Masks are among the most useful of skin care products. There are many different types of masks, each formulated for a specific purpose. Tightening masks help tighten and tone sagging skin, drawing masks absorb excess oils, and moisturizing masks add moisture to the skin. Depending on its formulation, a mask can soothe the skin, oxygenate it and improve circulation, nourish, help clear blemishes, or reduce fine lines and wrinkles for a short period of time. Masks can be either hard or soft.

■ Scrubs and peels are exfoliant products that basically work like super-cleansers to remove dead skin cells and remove impurities from the pores while stimulating and improving the circulation of the skin. Scrubs contain small granules of mild abrasives that remove dirt and dead cells when they are rubbed off the skin. They leave the skin clean and glowing.

■ Peels contain enzymes that digest the dead skin cells. They do not have an abrasive action. These enzymatic peels work on the surface of the skin and are safe to use. Chemical peels, however, remove layers of living skin and may be used only by dermatologists or other physicians.

■ Treatment products fall into a broad category that covers all those products that help normalize the skin function and help heal skin problems. *Note:* See a dermatologist to be sure you are using the right product for your skin condition.

■ Special purpose products cover a wide range of products designed to accomplish specific tasks. These can include such items as oil absorbers, which are made to absorb excess oil from the skin. They can include skin toners, which are designed to lighten the skin and even out skin coloration. If someone has uncovered a need for a product that performs a specific task, it is almost a sure thing that some company has developed a product to meet that need.

Product States

Next, consider the product state. What form does the product take? This is important because it affects how the product is used. Products are available in a number of different forms: liquids, creams, lotions, gels, solids, aerosols, and so on. Liquids flow freely and are pourable. They tend to be clear. Creams tend to be thicker and are usually emulsified and are generally opaque. Creams are usually spreadable. A pourable cream is a lotion, which is not as thick. Gels are thick and sticky, with a jelly-like consistency. They are not usually emulsified and can be clear or transparent. Solids can be loose and free flowing, like powder, or they can be bound particles, as in sticks. They can vary in texture and in consistency. Some solid products are used in that form. Others are mixed with water or other liquid for use, as, for example, a wheat germ mask, which comes as dry particles of wheat germ that are mixed with warm water to make a spreadable paste. Other solids are heated to change them into a liquid form for use, like a paraffin mask, where the solid paraffin wax has to be heated to about 134°, where it will flow onto the skin, before it can be used. As it cools down on the skin, it becomes a solid again. Aerosols let the user apply the product as a mist or a foam. In a mist, the product is broken into tiny droplets and dispersed by a propellant. In a foam, the product mixes with the propellant to form a fluffy, light, aerated mass.

You cannot consider the product contents or function without also considering how it is packaged. In many cases, the chemicals in the product will determine its form and its packaging. No matter what form the product takes, it has to be packaged in some way. The packaging is an important part of the product. It lets the product be stored. It protects the product. It identifies the product. And it allows access to the product. Especially for retail sales, it makes the product attractive.

Like the products themselves, the packaging can take a number of forms: bottles, jars, cans, boxes, tubes, ampules, and so on. Bottles are used for pourable liquids and lotions. Jars and cans are for creams and loose solids. Boxes hold bound solids, and tubes contain pastes and gels. Ampules are small hermetically sealed glass tubes that contain a concentrated active ingredient.

Regardless of type, the package performs a number of functions. It has to keep the product clean and sanitary, so it must be relatively impervious to the outside. In the case of just about all but bound particle solids, the package should not let in air, moisture, or contaminants, nor should it let the product leak out. If the product is sensitive to light, the package should be opaque or transparent dark brown or green. The package should be reclosable. With ampules, for example, once one is opened, the entire contents must be used.

The package should allow ready access to the contents, that is, it should make the product easy to use. If you cannot get the product out of the container in the amount needed when needed, the package is not functional.

The key product questions still remain, however. What is in the product? What ingredients does it contain? And even more importantly, what do these ingredients do? What do they accomplish?

PRODUCT INGREDIENTS

All products consist of one or more ingredients. Hopefully, the manufacturer has chosen those ingredients to formulate the best possible product. Regardless of how many ingredients may be in a product, each should contribute something to its functioning. All ingredients should be compatible, that is, they have to work together and not fight each other. They also should be mixed correctly.

Ingredients can be divided into two main groups: active ingredients and formulation aids. Active ingredients are substances that actually do the work the product is supposed to do—the cleansing, the toning, the normalization, and so on. Formulation aids are substances that help the active ingredients do their work and provide important characteristics to the product.

Active Ingredients

Active ingredients are the substances that do the actual work. In terms of composition, they may be natural, that is, derived from animal, vegetable, or mineral components, or they may be synthetic, that is, manufactured. Regardless of their composition, they are all chemical. In terms of quantity, they may or may not be the major ingredients in the product. In fact, they will rarely be the major ingredients in the product. With few exceptions, there will be more formulation aids in a product than active ingredients.

- Cleansing agents, for example, soaps, detergents, skin cleansers, shampoos, do the actual work of cleaning the skin or hair by softening dirt and loosening its hold on the skin or hair so it can be rinsed away. Cleansers include sodium laureth sulfate and lauroamphocarboxyglycinate.

- Emollients soften and soothe by lubricating the skin. They also help hydrate the skin. There are a great many emollients. Some of the more popular ones include aloe vera, a botanical agent; lanolin, an animal agent; and cetyl acetate and myristal myristate, synthetic agents.

- Exfoliants can be considered supercleansers. They soften and remove (or aid in the removal of) dead skin cells from the surface of the skin. The AHAs, alpha-hydroxy acids, are currently widely used.

- Healing agents promote healing or soothing of the skin, provide antiseptic properties, and reduce or help prevent inflammation. Commonly used healing agents include herbs such as aloe, chamomile, and yarrow; vitamins such as biotin and retinol; minerals such as zinc oxide; and synthetic materials such as urea.

- Moisturizing agents help the skin absorb and retain moisture. Aloe and safflower oil are examples.

- Protectants do just what the name implies. They protect the skin from harm. Sunscreens are an example.

Formulation Aids

When it comes to formulation aids, the list is even longer and more varied. In almost any given product, there will be more formulation aids than active ingredients. They are just as important as the active ingredients. Without these substances, the product would lack many of the properties that make it work and, sometimes more importantly, make it easy to use.

- Antioxidants prevent spoilage caused by exposure to oxygen. Commonly used antioxidants include tocopherol (vitamin E) and benzoic acid. Some formulation aids can also function as active ingredients. Antioxidants, for example, can scavenge free radicals from the skin, and thus, act as protectants or healing agents.

- Binders hold the ingredients together and increase the consistency of the formulation. Sorbitol and glycerin are often used for this purpose.

- Buffers control the level of acidity or alkalinity during formulation by preventing wide swings in pH. Commonly used buffers include citric acid and calcium carbonate.

- Clarifiers remove unwanted materials to make them clear. Citric acid and tannin are commonly used.

- Colorants give the product its characteristic color. A wide variety of vegetable, animal, or mineral dyes or pigments are used. These may be used without specific government approval. Coal tar derivative dyes, however, must undergo a certification process before they can be used in skin and beauty care products. Certified colorants are listed as FD&C (food, drug, and cosmetic) colors, which can be used in foods as well as in drugs and cosmetics; D&C colors, which cannot be used in food, but can be used in drugs or cosmetics; or ext. D&C colors, which may be used only for external use in drugs and cosmetics.

■ Defoaming agents keep the ingredients from foaming during formulation. Simethicone is one of the most widely used defoamers. This chemical is the main active ingredient in many over-the-counter remedies for excess gas.

■ Deodorizers eliminate unpleasant or unwanted smells. Chlorophyll and urea are often used for this purpose.

■ Emulsifiers let oil and water be mixed together to form an emulsion. Commonly used emulsifiers include glyceryl stearate, polysorbate 80, and triethanolamine (TEA).

■ Extenders increase the volume of the product and dilute the product. Water and petrolatum are two examples.

■ Fixatives retard the vaporization of the components of fragrances, making the desired odors last longer. Musk and civet are commonly used as fixatives.

■ Foaming agents are added to products, usually cleansers and shampoos, to make them foam during use. Dodecylbenzene sulfonic acid is one example.

■ Fragrances give the product its characteristic odor. A wide variety of natural and synthetic fragrances are used. They operate on three levels. The first impression, or top note, of the fragrance is the most volatile and vaporizes first. The major characteristics of the fragrance are in the second level, or body note, which vaporizes more slowly. The third level, or bottom note, is what is left after the volatile components of the fragrance have vaporized. Fragrances are made up of complex blends of ingredients and are normally regarded as proprietary, that is, trade secrets, of manufacturers. They are the only ingredients in a product that do not have to be listed on the label.

■ Humectants retard moisture loss in the product while it is in the container and also help trap moisture on the skin. Glycerin, sorbitol, and propylene glycol are widely used.

■ Lubricants provide a coating on the skin to reduce friction and wear. Mineral oil, cocoa butter, and isopropyl myristate are common lubricants.

■ Opacifiers make the product milky, so that light is not transmitted through it. Cetyl alcohol and stearyl alcohol are often used for this purpose.

■ Preservatives kill harmful bacteria, fungi, and yeasts, increasing the shelf life of the product and keeping it safe to use. Isothiazolone, methyl paraben, and imidazolindyl urea are among the preservatives in the formulators' arsenal.

■ Sequestering agents retard changes in the appearance of the product, especially in color or texture. Although they are a type of preservative, they work by chemical action as opposed to attacking microorganisms. Tetrasodium pyrophosphate (TSPP) and ethylenediamine tetraacetic acid (EDTA) are common sequestering agents.

■ Solvents dissolve or disperse the other ingredients in a product. Water is the most common solvent. Alcohol, acetone, and methyl ethyl ketone are also used.

■ Stabilizers maintain the equilibrium of the product and keep its characteristics from changing. Among the many stabilizers used in skin care products are borax, polysorbate 80, and cetyl alcohol.

■ Surfactants reduce the surface tension of the product and allow the product to spread and penetrate more easily. They are also called wetting agents. Sodium laureth sulfate and dioctyl succinate are two of the most commonly used surfactants.

■ Texturizers enhance the texture of products, that is, they make the products smoother. Calcium chloride and biotin are commonly used.

■ Thickeners give body to the product. Among the commonly used thickeners are bentonite, carbomer 934, stearic acid, and cellulose gum.

■ Vehicles are carriers for the other ingredients and, in most cases, account for the largest portion of the product. Water is the most commonly used vehicle, although alcohol or other solvents are also used.

Product Labeling

By law, all cosmetic products must list all ingredients on the label, except for specific fragrances. Ingredients are listed in descending order according to the amount of the ingredient contained in the product. Actual amounts do not have to be listed.

Labels are important. In many ways, they are the primary source of information about a product and what goes into it. So it is important to know how to read product labels. For example, here is a list of ingredients on the Dr. Thrower Dry Skin Cleanser. According to the label, the cleanser contains: water, isopropyl palmitate, glycerin, stearic acid, TEA, cetyl alcohol, sodium lauryl sulfate, EDTA, methylparaben, propylparaben, diazolidinyl urea, carbomer, sodium benzoate, and fragrance.

■ Water, the ingredient present in the greatest quantity, is the vehicle. It carries the rest of the ingredients, dispersing them evenly throughout the product.

■ Isopropyl palmitate is an emollient and moisturizer to soothe and soften the skin. It is derived from coconut or palm oil.

■ Glycerin is a humectant that helps the skin retain water. It also helps the cleanser spread evenly.

■ Stearic acid is an emulsifier and thickening agent. It is one of the main ingredients in soap.

- TEA (triethanolamine) is also an emulsifier. It helps adjust the pH of the cleanser.
- Cetyl alcohol acts as both an active ingredient and a formulation aid. As an active ingredient, it is an emollient that helps soothe and smooth the skin. As a formulation aid it is an emulsifier and a thickener.
- Sodium lauryl sulfate is the primary cleansing agent in the cleanser. It is a foaming agent and a dispersant and also acts as a surfactant.
- EDTA (ethylendiamine tetraacetic acid), methylparaben, propylparaben, diazolidinyl urea, and sodium benzoate are preservatives. Diazolidinyl urea is also a deodorizer and antiseptic.
- Carbomer is a cross-linking agent that stabilizes the emulsion and helps keep the particles in suspension.
- Fragrance gives the product a pleasant aroma.

Product Modes of Action

It is also necessary to understand the modes of action of the various products used. Products, and their ingredients, work in three ways: chemically, mechanically, and psychologically. All three modes are equally important to a product's effectiveness.

Products work chemically as they undergo chemical reactions with and within the body, as when a healing agent reacts with an inflammation to reduce the pain and soothe the skin or when a cleanser reacts with dirt and sebum to loosen their hold on the skin.

Products work mechanically as they coat the skin to trap moisture or develop heat from friction as they are rubbed onto the skin.

Products work psychologically as they make you feel better and provide a sense of well-being. The products are comfortable and soothing. The psychological effects of the products used or the services provided should not be underestimated.

Characteristics of a Good Product

What makes a product good? A good product has seven major attributes:

1. Effectiveness—it actually works and does what it is supposed to do.
2. Reliability—it works the same way every time; it can be counted on to do its job.
3. Ease of Use—it is easy to store, easy to apply, and easy to remove. It has clear, concise directions for best use. In short, it does not require more work than is necessary.
4. Cost Effectiveness—it is affordable to use. It has a long enough shelf life so it can be purchased in reasonable quantity and stored without spoilage. It gives excellent value for the money spent.
5. Safety—it will not harm users, as long as it is used properly and directions for use are followed.
6. Pleasantness—it smells good, looks good, and is enjoyable to use.
7. Salability—the operator can make a profit on the product.

THE FDA AND THE FTC

It is also important to understand the role of the Food and Drug Administration (FDA) and Federal Trade Commission (FTC). They are two federal agencies that greatly affect the beauty business. The FDA is responsible for monitoring the safety and effectiveness of cosmetics, food, and drugs and seeing that these products meet the standards of the Food, Drug, and Cosmetic Act. It tests and approves products and has the authority to remove products from the marketplace. The agency can also challenge claims made by manufacturers about the products and can demand substantiation of those claims. It is also responsible for monitoring the truth and accuracy of claims made on packaging and on labels.

The FTC enforces laws that prevent unfair competitive practices in business. It is also responsible for stopping the manufacture and sale of counterfeit products, which is a big problem in the beauty industry. Although the FTC does not get involved in products otherwise, it can demand substantiation for claims made in advertising.

One area the FDA gets involved with is defining the difference between a cosmetic and a drug. What is the difference? This is an important consideration for estheticians and consumers. Cosmetologists can use cosmetics on clients. They cannot use drugs. Drugs are the jealously and zealously guarded tools of the medical community.

In the most simple terms, *cosmetics* are products that remain on the surface of the skin or at most, penetrate only into the epidermal layer of the skin. *Pharmaceuticals* (drugs) penetrate into and beyond the dermal layer of the skin and are absorbed into the bloodstream. Cosmetics beautify. Drugs cure. Cosmetics do not significantly or permanently alter the skin's structure or function, or affect any body function beyond the skin. Drugs do significantly and permanently affect body functions.

All cosmetics are used topically, that is, they are applied to the surface of the skin. Drugs are used topically and are ingested, that is, they may be taken internally. But a cosmetic can contain ingredients that are classed as cosmetic when used in a beauty aid but classed as a drug when taken internally. Take, for example, salicylic acid, an ingredient in some skin cleansers. As the major ingredient of aspirin, taken internally, it cures a headache.

The key to the difference is skin penetration. Do cosmetic products actually penetrate into the skin? The answer is a qualified yes. Although the skin is a relatively impermeable barrier, if the molecular structure of the product is small enough, it will penetrate the skin, at least into the epidermal layer. If the molecules are too large, the product will not penetrate. But a skin care product does not have to penetrate the skin to be effective. Most products are designed to work on the skin's surface and they do the job admirably.

The line between cosmetics and drugs has become thinner and thinner as new advances in technology have been made. It is important not to cross that line. Many cosmetic manufacturers are carefully walking that line now. In fact, many of the claims they make for their cosmetic products—if they were true—would have the FDA classify them as drugs.

PRODUCT CLAIMS—MYTHS AND MISCONCEPTIONS

It is vital to look at product claims carefully. Keep in mind that most manufacturers are ethical in their business dealings and genuinely try to make truthful claims about the products. In most cases, they actually believe the claims they make because they can show scientific proof that the claims are true. But they are driven by a need to generate a profit on the products and are pushed by competitive pressures to exploit fads in the cosmetics business and to show their products are better than the competition's.

The reader should keep an open mind and give the manufacturers the benefit of the doubt as to their integrity, but should take what they say with a grain of salt until the truth of the claims can be verified. Intelligent users should also know that miracles do not come in bottles or jars. There is an old adage that holds just as true with products. "If it sounds too good to be true, it isn't true."

What are some of the current fads in the beauty industry that are fueling product proliferation and claims for those products? Are those claims true or false? Or are they just misleading?

"Our products are all natural and chemical free." First, there is no such thing as a chemical-free product. Remember what was said before. Everything is chemical, whether it is natural or not. All matter is composed of chemicals. As to the all-natural claim—just because something contains herbs does not make it automatically natural. Read the label. Are there preservatives in it? Is the herbal content from herbal extracts? What about the other ingredients?

Even if something were to be all natural, that is no guarantee of quality or effectiveness. Some of the most virulent poisons are all natural. Poison ivy, for example, is all natural.

"Our product is not tested on animals." This claim is probably true, but just what does it mean? All the manufacturer is saying is that the finished product was not tested on animals. However, many of the ingredients in the product have been tested on animals. If they were not, the FDA would not allow their use. Some ingredients fall into an FDA classification GRAS, or generally recognized as safe. Others, however, have to undergo rigorous testing before the FDA will let them be used. Up to now, at least, the FDA will recognize as valid only tests conducted on animals. So, is the manufacturer's claim true? Yes. Is it meaningful? Probably not.

"Our product is hypoallergenic." All this means is that the product does not contain a fragrance. Countless tests and studies have shown that the major cause of allergic reactions in cosmetic products results from the fragrances they contain. Removing the fragrance lessens the likelihood of allergic reactions and the manufacturer can call the product "hypoallergenic." It does not mean that you cannot have an allergic reaction to the product. If you are allergic to anything in the product, you will have an allergic reaction. This is the reason patch tests should be conducted, even with hypoallergenic products.

"Our products fight aging." The single greatest cause of premature skin aging, which is what is most often seen, is overexposure to UV radiation, whether from the sun or from a tanning booth. If the skin is shielded from the radiation, aging will be retarded. If a manufacturer puts a sunscreen in the product, the FDA allows the claim that the product is antiaging. As a result, it is getting harder and harder to find cosmetic products without a sunscreen in them, even when the only reason for that ingredient is to support the claim of antiaging. After all, why is it necessary to put a sunscreen in a night cream?

"Our products are alcohol free." When most people think of alcohol, they think of rubbing alcohol or liquor. But alcohol takes many forms. Cetyl alcohol, for example, is a waxy solid that has none of the characteristics of its more widely known cousins. Unfortunately, alcohol is currently out of fashion in cosmetics, with the result that many manufacturers are touting alcohol-free products, even when no alcohol would have been used in the product in the first place. Keep in mind, though, that alcohols and their derivatives are important in cosmetic manufacture. Aldehydes, ketones, organic acids, and esters are all made from alcohol. So a product may be alcohol free, but ingredients may have come from alcohol.

"Our products are preservative free." They better not be! Not if you expect to use them safely or keep them stored for any length of time. Preservatives are essential for just about any type of product in use. They are what keep funny looking little things from growing in the bottle while it sits on the shelf. The only ways a manufacturer can keep from adding preservatives to products are to either keep them in refrigerated storage, keep them in sterile containers such as ampules, or to use ingredients that have built-in antiseptic properties. Another note, the more natural a product is, the more susceptible it is to microbial contamination, and the more it needs a preservative.

"Our products get rid of unsightly wrinkles." This is not totally true. No cosmetic product can permanently erase wrinkles. The best they can do is to make wrinkles less evident or to hide them temporarily.

"Our product contains alpha-hydroxy acids." The alpha-hydroxy acids, AHAs, are the current industry darlings. Virtually every manufacturer has jumped on this bandwagon. The term *alpha-hydroxy acid* covers a variety of organic acids derived from fruit and other sugars. The most commonly used AHAs are glycolic acid from sugar cane, lactic acid from milk, and citric acid from citrus fruits. Others include malic acid from apples and tartaric acid from wine. They represent a class of chemicals that seem to have outstanding emollient and soothing effects on the skin and are excellent exfoliants. Like any product, though, they need to be used properly and carefully. They are acids and, like any acid, can burn the skin if not used correctly.

The AHAs do a great job, but for best results they have to be used in fairly high concentration, which limits their use by anyone other than physicians. In cosmetic preparations, the concentration is limited by law. As a result, the effectiveness of these products is limited, although they are valuable tools in the hands of a competent esthetician. The problem is that they are so popular right now that manufacturers are making products containing AHAs, even in products such as cleansers, which are rinsed off the skin before the AHA has much chance to do any good at all. Here is an example of a potentially good product being overcome by too much hype.

CHAPTER 4

Herbs, Essential Oils, and Sea Products

Herbs, essential oils, and sea water and products from the sea are widely used ingredients in skin care products. A wide variety of these ingredients are available to the skin care product manufacturer. Each of these ingredients has specific uses. As a result, it is necessary to have a basic understanding of the principles involved in these products because of their impact on the care of the skin.

HERBS

The use of herbs (i.e., plant materials) has its roots in antiquity. Every culture, even the most primitive, has a history of herbal medicine. Today, herbs are widely used throughout the world. Whether used as spices, cosmetics, or medicine, herbs play an important part in everyday life. Although the medical use of herbs has declined in our modern technological societies in favor of allopathic medicine, which relies on synthetic drugs, herbs remain valuable homeopathic remedies.

Hundreds of different herbs are used both singly and in combinations. Collectively, these herbs have a variety of properties. They soothe or stimulate, moisten or dry, tighten or ease. They heal, alleviate pain, dispel gas, cleanse, and purify the blood. They arouse or diminish sexual desire. They are antiseptic, antibiotic, and disinfectant. They increase perspiration or decrease it. The list could go on and on.

As medicines, herbs detoxify, normalize, or build. Detoxifying herbs eliminate poisons from the body and help purify it. Normalizing herbs help correct imbalances in bodily functions that result in illness; thus, they let the body heal itself as opposed to synthetic drugs, which alleviate symptoms but may not eliminate the underlying cause of the illness. The building herbs strengthen the various organs of the body to help prevent further illnesses.

As homeopathic remedies, herbs work slowly. Allopathic remedies, that is, synthetic drugs, work quickly. As an analogy, consider an illness as a mountain. There are two ways to level a mountain. It can be eroded by the action of rain and the elements slowly but gently, with no traces left or it can be blasted apart with dynamite, quickly but roughly, with rubble strewn about. Although they work slowly, herbs are thorough yet gentle and, for the most part, have few undesirable

45

side effects. Synthetic drugs, on the other hand, work rapidly, but are rougher on the body's systems and can have a number of undesirable side effects.

Retinol A, for example, a widely used drug for treating acne, controls blemishes rapidly and effectively but has potentially harmful side effects, such as headache, nausea, and possible destruction of sebaceous glands. By careful use of skin care products that contain a variety of herbs, it is possible to control acne effectively, albeit more slowly, without side effects. The drug treats the symptom of acne, the excess sebum. The herbs treat the underlying causes of acne and bring the body functions into balance so the reasons for the excess sebum are eliminated.

Admittedly, this example is overly simplified. It is important to remember that allopathic remedies are valuable and should be used when warranted. Always follow the advice of a physician.

Herbs are available from many sources. They may be picked in the wild, but this requires considerable time and expertise. Similarly, they may be grown in home gardens. This also requires time. The more practical sources are the herb specialty stores and some manufacturers of skin care products.

Herbs are most effective when they are used fresh. The fresh plant consists of the root, stem, leaf, and in the case of the flowering plants, flower and fruit, and in the case of woody plants, bark. For a given herb, one or more parts of the plant may contain the active, or medicinal, ingredient. Fresh herbs must be used soon after they are picked because their effectiveness diminishes rapidly. For this reason, fresh herbs are harder to use.

To maintain long-term stability, herbs are often dried, then ground into powders for use. Although they lose some activity when dried, they remain efficacious for longer periods. They should be stored in dark, airtight containers to prevent moisture absorption that could cause them to spoil.

Herbs may be prepared in a number of ways: as infusions, decoctions, poultices, fomentations, tinctures, or ointments.

- An *infusion* is made by steeping the herb in boiling water, just as in making tea. (Herb teas are infusions.) The process of steeping extracts the vitamins and volatile ingredients from the plant. The liquid is then strained and can be taken internally or used externally.

- A *decoction* is similar to an infusion, except the herb is boiled in the water instead of being steeped. This process extracts the mineral salts and bitter principles from the plant. The liquid must be strained before using.

- A *poultice* is made by bruising or crushing the herb and mixing the pulpy mass with a hot liquid or gummy substance to make a paste. The paste can be applied directly to the skin or wrapped in a hot, moist towel and wrapped around the body part to be treated.

- A *fomentation* is made by soaking a towel in a hot infusion or decoction and applying it to the body part to be treated. Fomentations are less effective than poultices because the application of the active ingredient is less direct.

- A *tincture* is made by soaking the herb in alcohol. The alcohol extracts the active ingredient from the plant. Tinctures keep for long periods of time.

Tinctures meant for internal use must be made with grain alcohol. Those meant for external use only may be made with other alcohols.

■ An *ointment* is made by mixing the herb with a hot fat or petroleum jelly to make a thick cream or salve. The salve is spread on the area of the body to be treated. Ointments are for external use only.

Although herbs may be used both internally and externally, skin care is concerned only with the external applications.

Hundreds of herbs have application in skin care. It is beyond the scope of this chapter to cover any but the most commonly used plants. Different herbs have different properties and affect the skin in different ways. Some are astringent, some cleansing, some purifying, some healing. Some herbs tighten skin; others ease tightness; some stimulate; others soothe. Table 4-1 lists a number of commonly used herbs.

Many herbs perform more than one function. Also, many herbs work in synergy. Combining herbs produces effects far in excess of the effect of each herb individually. The sum of the herbal effectiveness is greater than the total of the parts. Because of their effectiveness, a number of herbs are used in commercial skin care preparations. Among the most commonly used herbs are:

Acacia, also known as gum arabic, is a small tree common to tropical Africa. The useful part of the plant is the gum that exudes from the stem. Acacia soothes and softens skin. As a gum, it often serves as a binder for other ingredients in skin care preparations.

Almond is a tree grown in many parts of the world. The kernels of the nut are the most useful part of the plant. Almonds are emollients that help smooth rough skin while moisturizing. Ground almond meal makes a good cleansing scrub.

Aloe vera is a spiny, cactus-like plant native to east and south Africa, although it is cultivated in other tropical areas. The leaves, from which the gel is extracted, are used. Aloe is healing and soothing. It helps reduce inflammation. It moisturizes the skin and helps slow the outward appearance of aging. This herb has become one of the most popular herbs used in skin care.

Arnica is a perennial plant found in the northern latitudes. The flowers and roots are the useful parts of the plant. Arnica helps skin function normally by stimulating circulation and helping remove waste materials. It is an astringent and aids in the healing process.

Balm, also known as balm mint, is a perennial plant found in the Mediterranean and Near East countries as well as in the United States. The leaves are the most important part, although most of the plant may be used as well. A member of the mint family, balm is, at the same time, both soothing and stimulating to the skin.

Birch, also called white birch, is a tree common to the northern United States and Canada. The bark is the most important part, although the young leaves may also be useful. The herb is soothing and healing and is an astringent. The active ingredient in birch bark is salicylic acid, the major component of aspirin.

Chamomile is a perennial plant found throughout Europe. The flowers are the important part of the plant. Chamomile softens and heals the skin and is an

TABLE 4-1	Commonly Used Herbs	
HERB	**PROPERTIES**	**REMARKS**
Acacia (gum arabic)	astringent, healing	tightening, stimulating, nourishing
Almond	cleansing, moisturizing	good antiwrinkle agent, blackhead remover
Aloe	healing, soothing, moisturizing, softening	good for all types of skin, especially dry skin
Arnica	astringent, healing	good for circulation
Balm mint	soothing, stimulating	
Birch	astringent, healing	good on damaged and blemished skin
Chamomile	astringent, soothing, cleansing, anti-inflammatory	good for blackhead removal, good antiwrinkle agent
Coltsfoot	healing, soothing	good on couperose skin
Comfrey	healing, softening cell regenerator	good for blackhead removal and damaged skin
Cucumber	astringent, drying, tightening	good for oily skin
Echinacea	astringent, healing	
Elder	healing, astringent, tightening	good for oily skin
Grape	soothing, healing	good for dry skin
Horsetail	astringent, tightening, drying, stimulating	good for oily skin
Houseleek	healing, nourishing	good for blackhead removal and on blemished skin
Lady's mantle	astringent, drying, healing, cleansing, anti-inflammatory	good for oily skin, good antiwrinkle agent
Lemon	astringent, drying, healing, soothing	good for oily skin and blackhead removal
Marigold	healing, moisturizing, softening, soothing	good for circulation, good antiwrinkle agent, good for couperose skin
Marshmallow	healing, soothing, softening	good on damaged skin
Rosemary	astringent, cleansing, stimulating, antiseptic	good for circulation
Sage	astringent, healing, tightening, soothing	good for oily skin
St. John's wort	astringent, healing, antiseptic	
Witch hazel	astringent, drying, antiseptic	
Wild Oregon grape	purifying, healing	good for blemished skin
Yarrow	astringent, drying, stimulating	good for oily skin and blackhead removal

astringent. The active ingredient in chamomile is azulene, an anti-irritant and anti-inflammatory agent.

Coltsfoot is a perennial plant found in wet areas in the United States and Europe. The leaves and the flowers are the important parts. Coltsfoot soothes and heals the skin. It acts on the capillaries near the surface of the skin, making it good for use on couperose skin.

Comfrey is a perennial plant common to the United States and Europe. The roots are the most important part of the plant. Comfrey softens the skin and helps heal wounds and bruises. It also helps stimulate tissue growth. The active ingredient of comfrey is allantoin.

Cucumber, the fruit of the common garden plant, is an important plant for skin care. Cucumber juice is an astringent that softens, moisturizes, and nourishes the skin.

Echinacea, a midwestern perennial plant, has antiseptic properties and is useful as a blood purifier. Like all herbs that purify the blood, echinacea can be effective for use on skin conditions such as eczema and acne. The root is the part of the plant used.

Elder, a shrub native to many parts of the world in a variety of forms, has healing properties. An astringent, it stimulates circulation and tightens skin. Roots, leaves, and flowers all contribute to skin care.

Horsetail is an annual plant native to North and South America. The leaves have astringent properties. Horsetail is stimulating and drying and helps tighten the skin. It helps promote elasticity and rejuvenates the skin.

Houseleek, a perennial European plant, is astringent and cooling. Juice from the leaves is healing and soothing for a number of skin conditions.

Lady's mantle, a perennial plant found in damp areas in North America and Europe, is healing and anti-inflammatory. It is an astringent and natural cleanser. The entire plant can be used.

Lemon, the citrus fruit common to Florida and California, is an effective astringent and cleanser for the skin. It has healing and drying properties and helps hydrate surface cells. Pure lemon juice may be too acidic for direct application to the skin and should be diluted with water.

Marigold, also known as calendula, is an annual garden plant. The leaves and flowers have antiseptic and healing properties and help soften skin. Marigold helps detoxify and nourish skin cells.

Marshmallow is a plant found in waste areas in Europe and North America. It is a lubricant and softener for the skin and has healing and soothing properties. The entire plant can be used.

Rosemary, a cultivated shrub, is an antiseptic and stimulant for the skin. It decongests surface tissue and helps heal the skin.

Sage, a perennial plant found in the Mediterranean area, is an astringent and antiseptic. It is healing and is effective in reducing perspiration. The leaves are the parts of the plant used medicinally. Sage and rosemary are common kitchen spices.

St. John's wort, a perennial shrub native to the east and west coasts of the United States, is an astringent and antiseptic with healing properties. It is useful on irritated or injured skin. The entire plant is used.

Wild Oregon grape is an evergreen shrub found in lower mountainous areas of the Pacific Northwest. The roots are effective as a blood purifier and, as such, can be effective with a number of skin conditions, including acne, eczema, and psoriasis.

Witch hazel, a shrub that grows in wooded areas in Canada and the eastern part of the United States, is one of the best known herbs used in skin care. The leaves and bark are astringent and antiseptic and have healing properties.

Yarrow, also known as milfoil, is a perennial plant found throughout the world. It is astringent and drying and stimulates the circulation, thus is used to help improve the functioning of the skin tissue.

ESSENTIAL OILS

Aromatherapy is akin to herbal therapy in that it is a branch of plant medicine. Like herbal therapy, aromatherapy is based on the use of plant materials. Rather than using the various parts of the plant, however, aromatherapy uses the essential oils derived from those plants. Aromatherapy is easier to practice than herbal therapy, because the essential oils are concentrated and penetrate the skin. As with herbs, essential oils should be used only externally.

An essential oil is a phytohormone, or plant hormone, and serves the same function in the plant that animal hormones serve in the human body. In the plant, the essential oil functions as a bactericide, assists in photosynthesis, is the agent that repels pests, and assists in cross-pollination. The characteristic smell of the plant comes from the essential oils it contains. The purpose of the odor is to attract insects that carry pollen from other plants. Once the plant is pollinated, it stops emitting the scent because it no longer needs to attract insects. The essential oils are then reabsorbed into the plant to serve other purposes.

Essential oils are soluble in fats or alcohols. They are highly volatile and aromatic. Oils are obtained from the plant in a number of ways. The most common method is steam distillation, in which the plant is steamed to separate the oil from the rest of the plant. Oils may also be extracted with solvents or they may be pressed out of the plant by applying pressure. Because essential oils are soluble in fats, two methods of extraction with fat are used. These are enfleurage, in which the plant is placed on beds of fat, where the oils are absorbed, and maceration, in which the plants are bathed in hot fat.

Essential oils have four basic properties that make them important in skin care:

1. They are germicidal.
2. They stimulate or calm.
3. They penetrate.
4. They contain phytohormones.

Essential oils contain aldehydes, esters, and phenols. They are natural antiseptics, germicides, and fungicides. All essential oils, regardless of their other characteristics, have this ability to kill bacteria and fungi. In many cases, they are more effective than man-made chemical antiseptics, yet, unlike the chemical substances, are generally harmless to human tissue.

Approximately 20 percent of all essential oils are soothing. These oils cause the blood vessels to constrict, thus slowing the flow of blood and oxygen. About 80 percent of all essential oils are stimulating; they cause the blood vessels to expand, thus increasing the flow of blood and oxygen. Because of their effect on the circulatory system, essential oils are helpful in correcting skin problems associated with poor circulation.

Essential oils also have the ability to penetrate the skin and be absorbed throughout the body. Thus, for example, an aromatherapy massage affects not only the skin, but also the organs beneath the skin in the areas in which the oils are placed. The essential oils can also act as carriers for other molecules designed to penetrate the skin.

TABLE 4-2	Commonly Used Essential Oils	
OIL	**PROPERTIES**	**REMARKS**
Basil oil	antiseptic, stimulating, decongesting	
Benzoin	soothing, healing	useful on red, dry, itching skin
Cajuput	antiseptic, soothing, healing	useful for acne and psoriasis
Chamomile	soothing, healing, anti-inflammatory	useful with sensitive skin
Eucalyptus	antiseptic, germicide	
Geranium	soothing, healing, anti-inflammatory, decongestant	useful on sores, burns, and dry eczema
Hyssop	healing	useful with eczema
Juniper	antiseptic, healing stimulating	useful for acne, weeping eczema, and psoriasis
Lavender	soothing, healing anti-inflammatory	useful for acne, eczema, and psoriasis
Neroli	soothing, healing	
Rosemary	healing, germicide	useful for sores and burns
Sandalwood	soothing, healing anti-inflammatory	
Ylang-ylang	soothing, antiseptic	

The phytohormones contained in the essential oils supplement the natural hormones in the body, helping them work more effectively.

Just as there are many herbs of use in skin care, so are there many essential oils of value. Table 4-2 lists a number of essential oils commonly used in skin care preparations. Many essential oils work best in combination, so that synergy becomes a factor. Essential oils may be purchased individually or in premixed combinations designed for use on various types of skin. Among the essential oils of value in skin care are:

Basil oil is greenish yellow in color and contains the active ingredient linalol. It is a general antiseptic and, like all essential oils, has disinfectant properties. It stimulates the skin and helps decongest pores.

Benzoin, from the gum of an east Indian tree, is reddish brown in color and contains benzoic acid as its active ingredient. Benzoin soothes the skin and helps promote healing for red, dry, or itching skin.

Cajuput oil, from a tree common to the Philippines and Malaysia, contains cineol and terpineol. It is a general antiseptic and healing agent and helps calm the skin. It is useful against acne and psoriasis.

Chamomile oil, blue to greenish blue in color, contains azulene as its principal active ingredient. Chamomile oil soothes the skin and helps promote healing. It is an excellent anti-inflammatory agent and is useful on sensitive skin.

Eucalyptus oil, a clear liquid, contains eucalyptol and tannin as its principal active ingredients. It is an effective bactericide and parasiticide and helps disinfect sores and wounds.

Geranium oil, a clear to light green essence, contains terpenes and linalol as its active ingredients. It is an anti-inflammatory agent and soothes and helps heal the skin. It is useful against sores and burns and is effective against dry eczema. Geranium oil can be used with any type of skin but is especially good on congested, oily skin.

Hyssop oil, a light yellow essence, contains borneol and cetone. It is a healing agent and is useful for various skin disorders, including eczema.

Juniper oil, light greenish yellow in color, contains borneol and terpineol. It is an effective antiseptic and healing agent, and stimulates the circulation. Juniper oil is useful against acne, weeping eczema, and psoriasis. It is also good for cleansing and toning oily skin.

Lavender oil, a clear liquid containing linalol and geraniol among its principal active ingredients, is one of the most useful essences. Lavender oil is a soothing and healing agent and has anti-inflammatory properties. It is useful for many skin disorders, including acne, eczema, and psoriasis. This essence is also effective in promoting cell regeneration and is often used in skin-rejuvenating agents. It may be used effectively on all skin types.

Neroli oil, also known as orange blossom oil, is a pale yellow liquid extracted from Seville orange flowers. Its principal active ingredients are linalol and geraniol. It has soothing and healing properties and is useful on all types of skin. Like lavender oil, neroli helps cell regeneration.

Rosemary oil, a clear liquid, contains pinene and cineol among its ingredients. It is a healing agent and parasiticide. It is useful as an astringent and toner for the skin, and is effective against burns and sores.

Sandalwood oil, a thick greenish yellow liquid, contains terpenes. This oil is one of the most useful essences for skin care and may be used on all skin types. It is an antiseptic and healing agent and is effective in relieving itching and inflammation. It also acts as an astringent.

Ylang-ylang oil, a light yellow liquid, contains geraniol, linalol, and salicylic acid. It is antiseptic and soothing to the skin. Although it can be used with any skin type, it is especially effective on oily skin.

SEA WATER AND SEA PRODUCTS

The use of sea water and sea products has a valuable place in skin care. Marine clays, algaes, and sea plants, as well as sea water itself can be used effectively to cleanse and revitalize skin tissue.

All life came from the sea. The composition of sea water is identical to the composition of the natural fluids of the body. Sea water contains, in the same proportions, all of the trace elements, vitamins, amino acids, and minerals that are necessary to sustain life. Table 4-3 shows the composition of sea water.

The human body contains 60 percent to 85 percent water, depending on age. Children's bodies contain up to 85 percent water; older peoples' bodies, down to 60 percent, as aging is partly a process of drying out. The body fluids consist of blood (about 5 percent), lymph (about 15 percent), intercellular fluid (about 25 percent), and interstitial fluid (about 25 percent). All cells continually bathe in water. This water closely resembles sea water.

The products of the sea—seaweed, algae, and sediments—also have beneficial properties, and are generally more readily available than sea water. Seaweed and algae accumulate and concentrate all of the materials contained in the ocean. One kilogram of seaweed (2.2 lb) contains the same mineral wealth as 10,000 liters

TABLE 4-3	Composition of Sea Water	
ELEMENT	**AMOUNT (G/L)**	
Chlorine	19.00	
Sodium	10.50	
Magnesium	1.35	
Sulfur	0.89	
Calcium	0.40	
Potassium	0.38	
Bromine	0.07	
Carbon	0.03	
Strontium	0.008	
Boron	0.005	
Silicon	0.003	
Fluorine	0.001	

(2500 gallons) of sea water. Sediments, such as peloids, a blend of mud and oyster secretions, and clays, also contain many trace elements and minerals.

The marine plants, as used in skin care, perform a number of vital functions. They remineralize and rehydrate the skin, helping to retain moisture. They contain phytohormones, which are compatible with human hormones, and thus, work in the same manner as essential oils and herbs. They are rich sources of iodine, which acts on the thyroid gland, helping it secrete more thyroxine, important to the body's immune system. Seaweed is helpful in treating acne. Because of its iodine content, however, seaweed should not be used by people who are allergic to shellfish or are acne prone.

Seaweed and algae stimulate circulation, thus aiding nutrition and detoxification of the cells. Clays and peloids, on the other hand, have a soothing and calming effect and help decongest pores. Sea products work especially well when used in conjunction with essential oils. Seaweeds and algae are also excellent dietary supplements.

In algae pack treatments, algae is mixed with sea water to make a thick paste. The paste is spread along the person's spine and covered with paraffin. He or she then lies under heat lamps for thirty to forty-five minutes. The spinal column is chosen as the site of the treatment because the spine contains the bones closest to the surface of the body and major arteries and veins pass along the column. The marine ions diffuse quickly and penetrate more rapidly into the body from this area.

CHAPTER 5

The Importance of Nutrition

The body relies on an adequate intake of quality nutrients to function properly. The skin is no exception. When nutrients are of good quality and are taken in sufficient quantities and in the proper balance, the skin is healthy. It will have good color and vitality, will have adequate moisture and sebum production, and will function normally. When some or all of the required nutrients are missing from the diet, the skin may appear dull and lifeless, with poor color and improper functioning. Only the nervous system consumes more nutrients than the skin. When the body is short of nutrients, preference goes to the nervous system, so the skin goes hungry.

Poor nutrition directly affects the health of the skin. It indirectly affects the skin. When other organs in the body malfunction, symptoms often manifest themselves in the skin. So, it is difficult to separate the effects of nutrition on the skin from its effects on the rest of the body.

It is important to understand the principles of nutrition and diet and how they affect the skin. Knowing how the various nutrients work, what they do and what happens when they are deficient, can help reach the root causes of skin problems.

THE NUTRITIONAL PROCESS

Think of the body as a factory. Like a manufacturing plant, raw materials are taken in, products are manufactured, and waste materials are thrown away. In the case of the body, the raw materials are the nutrients that come from food, water, and air. The food and water are ingested and pass through the digestive system; the air comes in through the lungs. The products manufactured are energy and tissue, resulting from the complex chemical process called metabolism. The waste products, carbon dioxide, feces, and urine, are eliminated through the excretory system. Like the manufacturing plant, the quality of the products is only as good as the raw materials that go into making them.

The nutritional process has three parts. The first is ingestion, the second is digestion, and the third is elimination. All three work together equally to fuel the body and keep it healthy.

In the first part, *ingestion,* food is chosen, prepared, and taken into the body. Good nutrition starts with the choice of food. Today, there is an almost infinite variety of foods from which to choose. Good foods contain the necessary nutrients to fuel the body. Foods that are poor in nutrients offer only empty calories. The better the food that is ingested, the better the nutritional process.

Preparation is also important. Good foods, improperly prepared, can lose much of their nutritive value. Overuse of pesticides, additives, and preservatives can lower the quality of the food, as can overcooking.

Digestion, the second part of the nutritional process, begins when the food is placed in the mouth. As the food is chewed, it is broken into smaller pieces that are easier to digest. Saliva, the first enzyme encountered in the digestive process, is secreted by the salivary glands in the mouth. These enzymes, proteins that act as catalysts to change other substances while retaining their own identity, start the breakdown of the food into a useable form.

After swallowing, the food travels down the esophagus to the stomach where gastric juices consisting of hydrochloric acid and other enzymes continue the breakdown of the food. The food becomes a liquid, called chyme. From the stomach, the chyme moves into the small intestine. The pancreas and the liver produce more enzymes that break the food down even further.

The nutrients digested from the food, in the form of glucose, amino acids, and fatty acids, are absorbed into the bloodstream and lymphatic system through the walls of the small intestine. From here, they are transported to the various organs where they are converted into energy or tissue by the process of metabolism.

The undigested portion of the food passes from the small intestine to the large intestine, where the third part of the nutritional process, *elimination,* starts. The waste products are then expelled from the body in the form of feces and urine.

Proper elimination is just as vital to the health of the skin as the other two parts of the process. The body has to rid itself of waste materials before they putrefy and spread toxins throughout the body.

The process by which the nutrients are converted into tissue or energy is called *metabolism.* There are two phases: anabolism, the chemical conversion of nutrients to build up tissue and body chemicals, and catabolism, the breakdown of nutrients to supply energy. Both phases occur simultaneously.

NUTRIENTS

Nutrients are the carbohydrates, proteins, fats, vitamins, minerals, and water contained in the food. Each type of nutrient performs a different function for the body, either providing fuel for energy, for building tissue, or for helping to regulate the processes of the body. The fuel value of a given nutrient is expressed in calories, a measure of the amount of heat produced when the nutrient is oxidized. Thus, high-calorie foods have more potential for producing energy than low-calorie foods.

Carbohydrates

Carbohydrates supply most of the body's energy needs, whether for the production of heat, to keep the body temperature constant; for mechanical energy, to enable the muscles to work; or for electrical energy, to allow the nervous system to work.

The principal carbohydrates are sugar, starch, and cellulose. Through the action of enzymes, the simple carbohydrate, sugar, and the complex carbohydrate, starch, are converted into glucose. The glucose is either used immediately for energy or is further converted into glycogen and stored in the liver or in muscle tissue. The rest is converted into fat and stored throughout the body for later use. Cellulose is not digestible, so is not useful for energy conversion.

Proteins

Protein provides the materials for building tissue and for the production of hormones and enzymes. When carbohydrates and fat are deficient, the metabolism burns protein as a source of energy. Like excess carbohydrate, excess protein is converted into fat and stored in body tissue. The first areas to be affected by protein deficiency are the skin, hair, and nails.

Amino acids, the building blocks of the body, are produced by the action of digestion of the proteins. The body needs twenty-two different amino acids. However, the body is capable of producing only fourteen of them. The other eight, called the essential amino acids, must come from food. All eight of these must be present in specific proportions for synthesis to occur. Because animal products (e.g., meat) generally contain all eight essential amino acids, they are called complete proteins. Fruits and vegetables are incomplete proteins because they generally lack one or more of these eight. So care must be taken to combine these foods to get the proper mix of the essential amino acids. Table 5-1 lists the amino acids.

Fats

Fats provide a concentrated source of energy. When fats are oxidized, they give up twice as many calories as carbohydrates and proteins. They also carry the fat-soluble vitamins. They are the slowest of the main nutrients to be digested.

Animal fats are saturated, that is, they cannot accept any more hydrogen atoms in their structural chain, and tend to be solid at room temperature. Vegetable fats are unsaturated, that is, they can accept more hydrogen atoms, and tend to be liquid at room temperature. Vegetable oils, however, can be hydrogenated by adding gaseous hydrogen under pressure to convert the oil into solid form.

Fatty acids give fats their characteristic taste and texture. During digestion, the fatty acids are split from the structural chain and pass through the intestinal wall into the bloodstream. Three of the fatty acids—linoleic, arachidonic, and linolenic—are collectively known as vitamin F and are discussed in more detail in the section on vitamins.

Vitamins

Vitamins, certain organic substances found in food, are essential to life and health, even though they do not provide energy or build tissue like the three major nutrients. Vitamins are catalysts that help manufacture enzymes and regulate the metabolism so the carbohydrates, proteins, and fats can do their work. Because the body can form very few of the vitamins on its own, they must be supplied through the diet. There are at least twenty vitamins known at present. Some are water soluble; others are fat soluble. Table 5-2 lists the vitamins.

TABLE 5-1	Amino Acids
AMINO ACIDS	**FORMULA**
Alanine	$H_7NC_3O_2$
Arginine	$H_{14}N_4C_6O_2$
Asparagine	$H_8N_2C_4O_3$
Aspartic acid	$H_7NC_4O_4$
Cystine	$H_{11}N_2S_2C_6O_4$
Glutamic acid	$H_9NC_5O_4$
Glutamine	$H_{10}N_2C_5O_3$
Glycine	$H_5NC_2O_2$
Histidine	$H_9N_3C_5O_3$
Hydroxylysine	$H_{14}N_2C_6O_3$
Hydroxyproline	$H_{10}NC_5O_3$
Isoleucine*	$H_{13}NC_6O_2$†
Leucine*	$H_{13}NC_6O_2$†
Lysine*	$H_{14}N_2C_6O_2$
Methionine*	$H_{11}NSC_5O_2$
Phenylalanine*	$H_6NC_9O_2$
Proline	$H_{10}NC_5O_2$
Serine	$H_7NC_3O_3$
Threonine*	$H_9NC_4O_3$
Tryptophan*	$H_8N_2C_{11}O_2$
Tyrosine	$H_7NC_9O_3$
Valine*	$H_{11}NC_5O_2$

*Essential amino acids

†Isoleucine and leucine have the same chemical formula but differ structurally.

■ Vitamin A, a fat-soluble vitamin, is found as preformed vitamin A in fish-liver oil, cream, and butter. It is found as carotene in green leafy vegetables and carrots. The body converts carotene to vitamin A for use. This vitamin is necessary for proper growth of the bottom layer of skin and is used in the treatment of acne. The Recommended Dietary Allowance (RDA) for vitamin A is 5000 international units (IU) for adults. Vitamin A can be toxic in extremely high doses.

■ Vitamin B complex, a group of water-soluble vitamins, are found in bacteria, yeasts, and molds. These vitamins are necessary for the conversion of carbohydrates to glucose, which is burned to provide the body with energy. They are also necessary for proper metabolism and for the nervous system. All of the members of this group are interrelated in their function and should be taken together. Brewer's yeast and green vegetables are good sources of the B complex vitamins.

TABLE 5-2	**Vitamins**		
VITAMIN	**COMMON NAME**	**SOURCE**	**REMARKS**
A		green leafy vegetables, carrots, fish-liver oil, butter, cream	important for skin; RDA–5000 IU; toxic in large doses
B *complex*			
B_1	thiamine	wheat germ, bran, brewer's yeast	important for skin
B_2	riboflavin	wheat germ, bran, brewer's yeast	important for skin
B_3	niacin	poultry, fish, peanuts, lean meat	important for skin
B_5	pantothenic acid	organ meats, egg yolks, whole grains	
B_6	pyridoxine	meat, whole grains	
B_{12}	cobalamin	organ meats, fish, dairy products	
B_{13}	orotic acid	whey, root vegetables	
B_{15}	pangamic acid	whole grains, seeds, brown rice	
Biotin		organ meats, egg yolks	also known as vitamin H
Choline		wheat germ, liver, egg yolk	
Inositol		whole grains, liver, citrus fruit	important for hair growth
Folic acid		liver, leafy green vegetables	also known as vitamin M
PABA		liver, wheat germ, yeast	important for skin; sunscreen
C	ascorbic acid	fruits, vegetables	important for skin; RDA–60 mg
D		fish-liver oils	RDA–400 IU
E	tocopherol	wheat germ oil, seeds, nuts, soybeans	important for skin; RDA–5–15 IU
F	fatty acids	vegetable oils, cod-liver oil	
K	menadione	kelp, leafy green vegetables	synthesized in body
P	bioflavonoids	citrus fruit, grapes, cherries	important for skin
T		egg yolk, sesame seeds	
U		raw cabbage	

- Vitamin B_1 (thiamine) is needed for the conversion of carbohydrates to glucose and is found in wheat germ and bran. Thiamine is synthesized in the body by the intestinal flora.

- Vitamin B_2 (riboflavin) is vital to cell respiration and is important to healthy skin. It is found in the same foods that contain the other B complex vitamins. Riboflavin may also be synthesized by the intestinal flora.

- Vitamin B_3 (niacin) is necessary for healthy skin and as a coenzyme for breaking down the major nutrients. It is found in lean meats, poultry, fish, and peanuts. The body also converts the amino acid, tryptophan, into niacin.

- Vitamin B_5 (pantothenic acid) is needed for healthy skin and is important in cellular metabolism. It also helps retard aging and wrinkling. It is found in organ meats, egg yolks, and whole grains. Pantothenic acid is also synthesized by the intestinal flora.

- Vitamin B_6 (pyridoxine) aids in the production of hydrochloric acid and helps linoleic acid, one of the essential fatty acids, work better. It is also needed for the synthesis of DNA and RNA. This vitamin is found in meat and whole grains.

■ Vitamin B_{12} (cobalamin) contains mineral elements and is needed for proper metabolism. It is found in organ meats, fish, and dairy products. Unlike other vitamins, vitamin B_{12} cannot be produced synthetically. Vitamin B_{12} is also injectable.

■ Vitamin B_{13} (orotic acid) helps in cellular restoration and is used in the production of folic acid and vitamin B_{12}. It is found in whey and in root vegetables.

■ Vitamin B_{15} (pangamic acid) helps cell respiration and is needed for the metabolism of protein. It is found in whole grains, seeds, and brown rice.

■ Biotin, sometimes called vitamin H, is a coenzyme that aids the production of fatty acids and is essential for proper nutrition. It is found in organ meats and egg yolks.

■ Choline is necessary for a healthy liver and kidneys and for the absorption of fat by the body. It is found in lecithin, liver, wheat germ, and egg yolk.

■ Inositol works with choline in the metabolism of fat. It is also important to hair growth. Inositol is found in lecithin, whole grains, liver, and citrus fruits.

■ Folic acid, sometimes called vitamin M, helps in the formation of red blood cells and in the formation of nucleic acid. It also helps the liver function properly. Folic acid is found in liver and in green leafy vegetables.

■ Para-aminobenzoic acid (PABA) helps the intestinal flora produce folic acid and is important to the health of the skin. PABA is also effective as a sunscreen. It is found in liver, wheat germ, and yeast.

■ Vitamin C (ascorbic acid) is a water-soluble vitamin. It is less stable than the other vitamins and is oxidized easily. It is found in most fruits and vegetables, especially in citrus fruits. Vitamin C is important to the maintenance of collagen and the formation of connective tissue. It also helps many of the other nutrients function properly. In addition, vitamin C helps combat stress and acts as a natural antibiotic. Unlike some other vitamins, humans cannot synthesize vitamin C, so the entire requirement for this vitamin must be supplied through the diet.

　　The RDA for vitamin C is 60 mg, although smokers may need additional quantities of this nutrient, because smoking destroys vitamin C. There is no toxicity from excessive intake of vitamin C, although some people may experience some side effects, such as diarrhea or a rash.

■ Vitamin D, the "sunshine vitamin," is fat soluble. It is synthesized in the body through the action of sunlight on the skin, and is also present in fish-liver oils. Vitamin D aids normal growth and bone formation and helps maintain stability in the central nervous system. The RDA for vitamin D is 400 IU. Extremely large doses of vitamin D can be toxic. Milk is generally fortified with synthetic vitamin D.

- Vitamin E (tocopherol) is fat soluble. It is found in wheat germ oil, whole raw seeds, nuts, and soybeans. Vitamin E is an antioxidant and helps prevent the breakdown of fatty acids and other vitamins and the formation of free radicals. This nutrient is also important to cellular respiration and helps increase stamina and endurance. It also helps prevent the formation of scars on the skin. The RDA for vitamin E varies from 5 IU for infants to 15 IU for adults. Although vitamin E is generally not toxic, it may be harmful to persons with high blood pressure. Vitamin E is also used as an ingredient in some topical skin care products.

- Vitamin F, which consists of the three unsaturated fatty acids, linoleic, linolenic, and arachidonic, is necessary for normal functioning of the glands and for the regulation of blood coagulation. The unsaturated fatty acids also lubricate cells and nourish skin cells. Linoleic acid is an essential fatty acid, that is, it cannot be synthesized by the body and must be supplied in the diet. The other two can be synthesized from linoleic acid.

  Although there is no RDA established for unsaturated fatty acids, it is generally recommended that linoleic acid make up about 1 percent of the daily caloric intake. Vitamin F is not toxic, but excessive consumption of fatty acids can result in weight gain. Food sources for unsaturated fatty acids include natural vegetable oils, cod-liver oil, and wheat germ.

- Vitamin K (menadione) is fat soluble and is manufactured in the body by intestinal flora. It is also found in kelp and leafy green vegetables. Vitamin K is important for proper liver function and for the formation of some of the chemicals required for various body processes. It also helps foster proper blood clotting. Natural vitamin K is not toxic although excessive doses of synthetic vitamin K can produce toxic symptoms. Because it is synthesized by the body, deficiencies are rare, so no RDA has been established. Other sources of vitamin K are yogurt, alfalfa, and fish-liver oils.

- Vitamin P (bioflavonoids) consists of a water-soluble group of nutrients that occur with vitamin C in many fruits and vegetables. These nutrients, which consist of rutin, hesperidin, citrin, flavone, and flavonals, are needed to allow vitamin C to be used effectively. They also help in the formation of collagen and strengthen capillary walls. No RDA has been established for the bioflavonoids and they are considered to be nontoxic. Food sources include citrus fruits, buckwheat, rose hips, grapes, and cherries.

- Vitamin T and vitamin U are little known and their use is not yet fully understood. Vitamin T assists in the blood coagulation process and is found in egg yolks and sesame seeds. Vitamin U, found in raw cabbage, helps heal ulcers. Because so little is known about these two vitamins, no RDA has been established for either of them.

Minerals

Like vitamins, minerals are essential to proper body functioning. Minerals are inorganic nutrients that let vitamins work. Without them, vitamins would be

TABLE 5-3	Minerals	
MINERAL	**SOURCE**	**REMARKS**
Calcium	bone meal, milk, soybeans, salmon	important to skin, RDA–800–1200 mg
Chlorine	salt	
Chromium	eggs, liver, mushrooms, brewer's yeast	
Cobalt	meat, sea vegetables, milk, shellfish	
Copper	seafood, liver, whole grains, legumes, leafy green vegetables	important to skin
Fluorine	seafood, cheese, fluoridated water	
Iodine	fish, sea vegetables	RDA–1 μg/ kg of body weight
Iron	organ meats, whole grains, leafy green vegetables	RDA–10–18 mg
Magnesium	green vegetables, whole grains, soybeans	RDA–300–350 mg
Manganese	whole grains, nuts, green vegetables, eggs	
Molybdenum	meats, cereals, dark green leafy vegetables	
Phosphorus	meat, poultry, fish, eggs, whole grains	RDA–800 mg
Potassium	leafy green vegetables, bananas, potatoes	important to skin
Selenium	organ meats, fish, brewer's yeast	important to skin
Sodium	salt	
Sulfur	eggs, meat, fish	important to skin
Vanadium	organ meats, seafood	
Zinc	meats, eggs, wheatgerm	important to skin

unable to function. All of the minerals needed by the body must be supplied in the diet. None can be synthesized by the body. In their pure mineral form, these substances are largely indigestible. Before the body can use them, they must be made digestible through the process of chelation, in which the mineral bonds with an amino acid. Table 5-3 lists the various minerals.

At present, eighteen minerals are known to be important to life. The most important—calcium, iodine, iron, magnesium, phosphorus, and zinc—have had RDAs established. The other twelve minerals—chlorine, chromium, cobalt, copper, fluorine, manganese, molybdenum, potassium, selenium, sodium, sulfur, and vanadium—though also important, have not had RDAs set.

■ Calcium is the most abundant material in the body. It operates in conjunction with phosphorus to form bones and teeth. It also helps maintain healthy skin and helps prevent sun damage to the skin. Sources of calcium are milk, dairy products, soybeans, salmon, and bone meal. The RDA for calcium varies from 800 to 1200 mg.

■ Chlorine is generally found combined with sodium or potassium in the form of sodium or potassium chloride, or salt. Chlorine is needed to regulate the acid-alkali balance of the blood and to help maintain intercellular pressure. Most chlorine is supplied through the ingestion of salt in the diet. Chlorine deficiency may lead to hair loss.

- Chromium is essential for the proper enzymatic action in metabolism and for regulating blood sugar levels. It is needed in small concentrations. Food sources include eggs, liver, mushrooms, and brewer's yeast.

- Cobalt, a component of vitamin $B_{12,}$ is necessary for proper cellular functioning. Meat, especially organ meats, sea vegetables, shellfish, and milk are food sources for cobalt.

- Copper is important to the skin, nerves, and blood. It helps the amino acid, tyrosine, function to pigment the skin and works with vitamin C to form elastin. In addition, it helps form the myelin sheaths around nerve fibers and assists the development of hemoglobin in the blood. Copper is found in seafood, liver, whole grains, legumes, and leafy green vegetables. Copper deficiency may inhibit healing of skin sores.

- Fluorine helps strengthen bones and teeth. Although needed in small quantities for good health, fluorine is toxic in high concentration. In the United States, most fluorine is supplied in fluoridated water. Food sources include seafood and cheese.

- Iodine is necessary for the proper functioning of the thyroid gland. This mineral helps regulate energy, control the metabolism, and influence growth and development. The RDA for iodine is about $1\mu g/kg$ of body weight. Pregnant women should ingest slightly higher amounts. The best food sources for iodine are fish and sea vegetables. Iodine deficiency may lead to dry hair.

- Iron is important to the quality of the blood. This mineral combines with copper to help produce hemoglobin, which carries the oxygen in the blood. In addition, iron helps form myoglobin in muscle tissue. The RDA for iron is between 10 and 18 mg. Women require more iron than men. Organ meats, whole grains, and leafy green vegetables are the best dietary sources of iron.

- Magnesium is essential to metabolism and the maintenance of a suitable acid-alkali balance. It also helps convert blood sugar into energy. The RDA for magnesium varies from 300 to 350 mg, the lower amount for men, the higher amount for women. This mineral is found in most foods, especially in green vegetables, soybeans, whole grains, and apples.

- Manganese helps activate a number of enzymes that promote the functioning of vitamins. It also helps feed nerves and brain tissue. Food sources of manganese include whole grains, nuts, green vegetables, and eggs.

- Molybdenum helps iron and copper function properly in the body. Meats, cereals, and dark green leafy vegetables are good food sources for this mineral.

- Phosphorus is second only to calcium in its presence in the body. Like calcium, phosphorus is necessary to proper growth and healthy bones and teeth. For best functioning, these two minerals should be combined in specific proportions. The RDA for phosphorus is 800 mg. All high-protein foods contain phosphorus. These include meat, poultry, fish, eggs, and whole grains.

■ Potassium works with sodium to help regulate the balance between intercellular and intracellular fluid. These two minerals also help equalize the acid-alkali balance and are important for muscle functioning. Potassium also helps promote healthy skin. Potassium is found in green leafy vegetables, bananas, potatoes, and whole grains.

■ Selenium is necessary to maintain elasticity in tissues and for reproduction. An antioxidant, selenium works with vitamin E to help retard aging. Organ meats, fish, brewer's yeast, and whole grains are food sources for this mineral.

■ Sodium, in addition to working with potassium, helps maintain the solubility of other minerals in the blood. It also helps produce hydrochloric acid in the stomach. Present in most foods, sodium is one of the few nutrients for which there is little chance of deficiency. Table salt is the principle source of sodium in the diet.

■ Sulfur, a component of keratin, is essential for healthy skin and hair. It also helps in tissue respiration. Eggs, meat, fish, and dairy products are good food sources for sulfur. Sulfur is necessary for a good complexion. It keeps the skin smooth and youthful and it keeps hair glossy and smooth.

■ Vanadium helps in the proper development of bones and teeth. It also helps iron function in blood formation. Food sources of vanadium include organ meats, seafood, and whole grains.

■ Zinc is important for the proper functioning of many vitamins and enzymes as well as for normal growth and development. It also assists the body's natural healing processes. Zinc is essential for healthy skin. The RDA for this mineral is 15 mg. Food sources include meats, eggs, wheat germ, and brewer's yeast.

Water

Water is probably the most important nutrient of all. A person can survive for weeks without food, but only for days without water. It comprises almost two-thirds of the body's weight and is a part of virtually every bodily process from digestion through elimination. Water carries the other nutrients through the body and carries the waste products from the body. It also helps regulate body temperature. The amount of water the body needs daily varies according to how much is lost due to activity and environmental conditions.

Water needs increase during exercise, in hot weather, and for the elderly. During exercise or in hot weather, water is lost through perspiration and respiration. This water must be replenished to prevent heat exhaustion or heat stroke.

Heat exhaustion results from high temperatures during exercise. It can also occur while a person is at leisure. It is also common among the elderly who take diuretics prescribed by their physicians. The symptoms of heat exhaustion include weakness, vertigo, nausea, and vomiting. Faintness may precede collapse. The person may have a gray color. The skin is usually cold and clammy. Onset is sudden, but the duration is brief. Treatment for heat exhaustion consists of placing the person in a cool environment and giving fluids by mouth. Intravenous fluids are seldom necessary.

Heat stroke is a serious condition that, if left untreated, can be fatal. It is common among the elderly who suffer from preexisting chronic diseases or who are using diuretics. Military recruits and athletes who are exposed to high temperatures during vigorous exercise, and who lose large volumes of water as a result, are also at risk of heat stroke. The symptoms of heat stroke include high body temperatures (greater than 106°F.), and the inability to sweat. The skin is hot and dry, the pulse is racing, respiration is rapid and shallow, and the blood pressure is low. Treatment must be immediate. The person should be placed in a cool environment. Clothing should be removed and he or she should be immersed in an ice bath. The skin should be gently massaged. Fluids should be administered orally and intravenously.

Nutritionists advise drinking 6 to 8 glasses of water daily. Tea, coffee, and alcohol do not count. These beverages act as diuretics and promote water loss. One ounce of alcohol, for example, uses 8 ounces of water for digestion.

Water lost during exercise must be replaced. Twelve to 16 ounces of water are required to make up for every 2 pounds lost while exercising.

Urine color is a good indication of the body's need for water replenishment. The urine should be pale yellow in color. If it is dark, the body needs more water, so water intake should be increased.

Sports drinks are currently popular. They are necessary for people who lose large volumes of water during exercise or work. These drinks contain sodium, which lets the body retain more water. Plain water does not contain sodium, so more plain water is required to replenish lost water.

A typical sports drink contains 50 to 100 mg of sodium per serving. The daily adult bodily requirement for sodium is 1100 to 3300 mg. For most Americans, the daily sodium intake is 10 to 60 times that necessary for good health. As a result, most people will not benefit from sports drinks because their daily sodium load is more than adequate.

GUIDELINES TO GOOD NUTRITION

Good nutritional habits are a vital part of the overall skin care regime. The U. S. Department of Health and Human Services has published a list of seven dietary guidelines that can serve as a model for this advice (*Nutrition and Your Health: Dietary Guidelines for Americans*).

1. **Eat a Variety of Foods.** Although most foods contain more than one of the nutrients needed for good health, no one food contains them all. The only way to ensure an adequate intake of nutrients is to eat a balanced diet that contains foods from the following groups: fruits and vegetables; cereals, whole grains, and grain products; dairy products, such as milk, cheese, and yogurt; meats, poultry, fish, and eggs; and legumes, such as beans and peas.

With a balanced diet, there will be little need for taking extra vitamins or food supplements, although some people, notably pregnant women, the elderly, or women of child-bearing age, may need additional nutrients.

Men's nutritional needs differ from those of women. Men need about 2300 to 2700 calories per day, whereas women require only 1600 to 2400. In addition, women need food that is richer in nutrients.

2. **Maintain an Ideal Weight.** Everyone has an ideal weight, at which all the body systems operate most efficiently and at which health is optimized. This weight is based on height, build, and metabolism. Significant deviation from this ideal weight can lead to a variety of disorders.

Obesity increases the risk of high blood pressure, high triglyceride levels, increased cholesterol, diabetes, and higher risk of heart attack and of strokes.

A program for weight loss, to have the best chance for success in the long term, can be based only on reducing the caloric intake and increasing the amount of exercise. Weight loss should be gradual, no more than 1 to 2 pounds per week. Unfortunately, there are no quick and easy ways to lose weight permanently. It takes an adjustment of dietary habits.

3. **Avoid Too Much Fat, Saturated Fat, and Cholesterol.** A high blood cholesterol level increases the risk of heart attack. Diets rich in fats and saturated fats tend to increase blood cholesterol levels in most people. To control the cholesterol level, it is wise to limit the intake of foods high in fats. Fat intake should be limited to about 30% of the calorie total.

Good low-cholesterol protein sources include lean meat, fish, poultry, dry beans, and peas. Organ meats and eggs are high in cholesterol but contain many vitamins, minerals, and other important nutrients, so should be eaten in moderation.

Butter, cream, and most shortenings are high in cholesterol, so their intake should be limited. Foods should be prepared by boiling, baking, or broiling, rather than by frying.

4. **Eat Foods with Adequate Starch and Fiber.** The energy the body needs is supplied by both carbohydrates and fats. If fat intake is limited, the intake of carbohydrates should be increased to maintain the required caloric level.

In general, a low-fat, high-carbohydrate diet is healthiest. Carbohydrates contain about half as many calories per ounce as fats. In addition, the energy from fats is stored in the stomach and hips where it becomes body fat. The energy from carbohydrates, however, is stored in the muscles and liver.

Complex carbohydrates provide energy along with other vitamins and minerals. They also increase the amount of fiber consumed in the diet. Diets higher in fiber reduce chronic constipation and may help reduce the risk of some forms of cancer.

Whole grain breads, cereals, pasta, fruits and vegetables, beans, peas, and nuts are good sources of starch and fiber.

5. **Avoid Too Much Sugar.** The average American consumes 130 lb of sugar per year, either through direct use or through sweeteners added to foods or naturally present in foods. The major dietary problem with added sugar is the risk of tooth decay. It is best to limit the use of white and brown sugar, honey, and syrups and to use moderation in the consumption of foods containing these substances.

6. **Avoid Too Much Sodium.** The body needs sodium to function properly. The amount needed is about 1000 mg/1000 calories consumed. One teaspoon of salt equals 3 g. The American diet, however, contains much more sodium than is needed. Most processed foods, many beverages, and many condiments contain large quantities of salt. In addition, many people add table salt to their food.

   Excess sodium consumption may lead to high blood pressure, which is a significant health risk. It is best to limit the use of salt to reduce the intake of sodium. Add only small amounts of salt during cooking and do not add salt to the food at the table. Limit the intake of salty foods, especially snack foods such as potato chips and pretzels. Use other herbs and spices for flavoring.

7. **Drink Alcohol Only in Moderation.** Alcohol has little or no nutritional value but is high in calories. In addition, alcohol alters the rate of absorption of some nutrients, making them less useful to the body. Heavy drinkers may, therefore, suffer from vitamin and mineral deficiencies. In addition, heavy alcohol consumption may lead to diseases such as cirrhosis of the liver and to some types of cancer and may cause birth defects. The high caloric content of alcohol makes it difficult to drink while on a diet.

   Alcohol consumed in moderation, 1.5 ounces of pure alcohol—that is, one or two mixed drinks, 8 ounces of wine, or 24 ounces of beer—per day, does not seem to be harmful to adults, however. So, drink only in moderation.

CHAPTER 6

Braiding and Sculpting Techniques

The following descriptions will provide you with the basic knowledge of the popular natural braid styles and techniques. The creative art form is unlimited, and the techniques offered here are fundamental and can be improvised to allow self-expression. As demand increases for the natural braided look, the more diverse styles will become.

But more importantly, you must be aware of the differences and options that are available. It is through the complete understanding of naturally textured hair and the variety of braid styles and, above all, the required hands-on experience and practice that will enable you to be among the best.

STYLE AND BRAIDING TERMS

As the braid industry becomes more popular, innovative braid stylists will create more beautiful styling options. The names may vary from state to state; however, it is necessary to highlight the featured styles.

The following is a general description of the beginning-level techniques:

■ **African Kurl (Twist Out)**

This style is achieved by using a double twist technique. The twisting technique is done wet in order to promote textures and waves. "Twist out" is the unravelling of the twist, adding fullness and a crimped effect.

■ **Afro**

This style can be achieved on long or short curly, kinky, or wavy hair. Hair that is cut and textured can vary in its final shape.

■ **Afro Weave**

This style is achieved by attaching textured hair on a **weft** to a designed cornrow basis. It is sewn with a cotton thread.

■ **Braids (single or individual braids)**

These names are interchangeable for most braid stylists across the country. These techniques are basic "free-hanging" braids with or without extensions. The braid is divided into three equal sections that are intertwined or weaved into one another.

■ **Casama Braids**

Large, single braids with a tight stitch; they are tapered and/or curved at the ends.

■ **Cornrows and Canerows**

Underhand three-strand braids, interwoven to lay flat on the scalp. They can be designed and sculpted into varying patterns with or without extensions.

■ **Flat Twist**

Two-sectioned braid, interwoven to lay flat on the scalp. It can be designed into varying patterns with or without extensions.

■ **Geni-Locs**

This style uses the single-braid technique and wrapping technique. Yarn is used on this two-step procedure. Yarn gives a matte finish to resemble locks.

■ **Goddess Braids**

A large inverted braid designed to lay flat on the scalp in varying design patterns. The free end is styled into an updo finished style.

■ **Locks, Dreadlocks**

Natural textured hair is intertwined and meshed together to form a single or separate network of hair.

■ **Nu-Locs**

This technique is done with yarn fiber giving the extension a matte finish like locks. A single-braid-based technique is used.

■ **Nubian Coils**

This technique is styled on naturally curly or textured hair. Hair is curled into a cylindrical shape with a comb or hands.

■ **Lin Twist**

This technique resembles the flat twist and is performed with lin fiber.

■ **Silky Twist**

Large sections like a cornrow base are rolled and gelled into a flat design pattern.

■ **Silky Wrap or Silky Loc**

This style is a two-step process. First, the braid extension is applied; then the synthetic hair is wrapped around the braid.

CORNROWS

There are many techniques to starting the traditional on-the-base braid known as the cornrow. The cornrow is created with a three-strand, on-the-scalp braid that uses an underhand "pick-up" technique. The fundamental of braiding starts with the basic cornrow. According to master braid designer Annu Prestonia, co-owner of Khamit Kinks in New York and Georgia and celebrity braid designer, cornrows are the foundation of all braid styles. "If you excel at the art of cornrowing, all other braiding techniques are at your disposal," says Prestonia.

To cornrow like a professional, you must be patient and practice. A skilled braider must take the time daily to practice cornrowing. Cornrowing is the repetition of the entire woven patterns; the sequence of weave patterns may vary and will determine the style. However, the series of revolutions are a simple repetitive motion of secure pick-up motion. Practicing on a mannequin will help to develop speed, accuracy, and finger-wrist dexterity. Braid services can vary in time from two hours for a large braid to two days for a micro braid. Mastering the basic cornrow technique will enable you to approach other braid styles with confidence.

Skillful cornrowing is designed through the process of sculpting the parted sections. Sculpting is more than just vertical or horizontal partings. When sculpting the braid, you must first visualize the finished look. This will allow you to create smooth and consistent curved partings that contour with the head. The curve partings are a part of the design, so they must be neat and even. The more creative you are in designing the parts, the more beautiful the finished sculpted look will be. This contouring or sculpting is especially beautiful on small to medium sized cornrows.

Three-Strand Cornrow

Finished style

Practice the following technique for cornrowing. It uses three strands with an underhand weaving motion, in which the strands on the sides are always passed under the center strand, alternating from the right side to the left, and left side to the right. Tulani Kinard, master braider and owner of Tulani's Regal Movement in New York, gives the following technique:

Divide the hair into three equal parts.

1. Begin by taking a section as small as you want the braid to be. Divide the section into three equal strands. Start at the hairline (depending on the style, the braid can begin anywhere from the nape of the neck forward). The strand on the far left will be called strand 1, the center is strand 2, and the strand on the far right is strand 3.

2. Cross the left strand 1 under center strand 2. Center strand 2 is now on the left and strand 1 is the new center. Passing the strand under the center with each revolution creates the underhand cornrow braid.

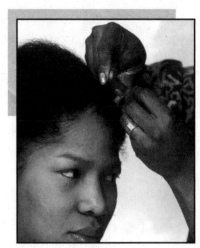

Cross strand 1 underneath strand 2.

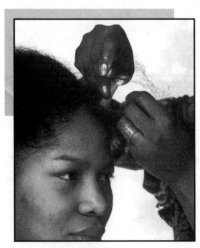

Cross strand 3 under strand 1.

3. With each crossing under, or revolution, you must pick up new equal-size sections of hair and add them to the center strand 2; pick up before crossing the outer strands under the center strand. Now cross strand 3 under strand 1. At the end of this revolution, strand 3 is the new center.

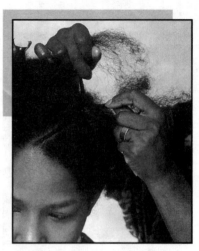

Pass strand 2 under strand 3. Work from side to side.

4. Each time you make a revolution (crossing under the center strand), you must pick up the hair from the scalp and add it to the new center. With each revolution, alternate the side of the braid on which you pick up hair.

5. As you move along the section, cornrowing and picking up more hair, you add fullness to the braid. The braids appear to be closer together. Contoured parting should be clean and neat.

Cornrows with Extension

Hair additions or extensions are used to lengthen short hair, to add volume to thin hair, to protect damaged hair, to add dimension to the height of the natural hair, to allow the braid style to last longer, and to make a creative and cultural statement.

The feed-in method can be applied to cornrows or individual braids. There are several different methods for integrating extension hair into the hairline. Some methods just introduce large amounts of extension material to the fragile hairline, leaving the front of the braid bulky and knotted. In some cases, this bulky, bumpy look has become very popular. It is a fast and effective method for adding extensions if one does not mind the braids looking like a helmet!

But many braid professionals contend that the braid extension should be concealed and the knot or lump eliminated because it is damaging to the hair. "When hair is braided using the knot or lump at the beginning of the braid, it is a telltale sign that you are wearing an extension," notes Taliah Waajid, author of *Hairitage Masterpieces*. She uses the feed-in method to gradually add hair throughout the braid. Literally, strand by strand the braid must be built up. Too large amounts of extension material places excessive weight on the fragile areas of the hairline. It also tightens and pulls the hair and creates an unrealistic finished look. By properly applying the correct tension application with the feed-in method, you can eliminate the artificial look.

The traditional cornrow does not look like a hat of braids. It is flat, natural, and contoured to the scalp. The parting is definitely important because it defines the finished style. The feed-in method creates a tapered or narrow base at the hairline. As small pieces or strips of extension hair are added, the base fills in, bringing the adjoining braids closer together.

This technique takes longer to perform. However, the cornrow lasts longer, looks more natural, and does not put excessive tension on the hairline. Practice this method for a flat contour, natural cornrow style:

1. Start at the hairline by parting off a cornrow base in the desired style.

2. At the starting point, no extension is added. If the hair extension is required because of a thinning hair-line, minute amounts can be applied (five to ten strands). This is all relative to the size of the cornrow.

3. Divide the natural hair into three equal portions.

4. With the first revolution, left strand 1 crosses **under** strand 2.

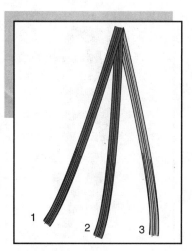

Three-strand extension

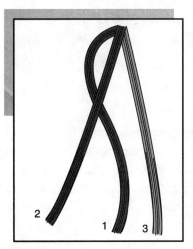

First revolution

5. On the second revolution, the right strand 3 crosses **under** strand 1. A small portion of natural hair is picked up and added to the outside portion during the revolution.

6. On the third revolution, bring strand 3 to the center strand, picking up a small portion at the base of natural hair.

Second revolution

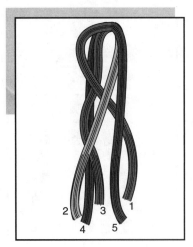

Third revolution

7. After several revolutions and pick ups, apply small amounts of folded extensions under the natural hair, to the center and outside portions. Hair extension must be tucked into the fold of the two adjoining portions. The amount of extension should be proportionately less than the size of the base.

8. The folded extension is always applied to the center and outside portions before the pick up. Do not forget to pick up natural hair with **each** revolution to execute on the base cornrow.

There are several different ways to start a cornrow and feed in extension pieces. Experiment with as many methods as you can. Different hairlines and styles require different methods.

Overdirecting Braid Extension

Precision parting and sectioning is vital to all braiding techniques. Parting will determine the direction of the braid. Clean and precise partings are required to create a strong braid base. Hair strands must never be overdirected or misplaced within an adjacent braid. If single strands are incorporated into another section outside of its own section, the hair will eventually break. Overextending the hair adds tension to the unsupported strand.

During the cornrow process, when picking up hair at the base, the hair directly underneath the previous revolution must be incorporated into the braid. The hair picked up must never come from another subsection or be extended up into the braid from a lower part of the braid.

The same is true when applying any braid technique. When creating an individual braid with extensions, start in the center of the subsection. Overextending or misplacing the beginning of the extension leaves the hair exposed and unsupported, which can led to breakage and traction alopecia. This is particularly true when adding extensions to the hairline. If the extension is not secure (two or three revolutions before picking up), the extension will move away from the point of entry. This pulled base around the hairline will definitely create breakage and eventually cause alopecia.

TIP!   *For professional finishing, always trim or remove split ends that may pop through the braid shaft. Hold scissors flat, moving up the braid shaft. Avoid cutting into the braid.*

Senegalese Twists

Finished style

Senegalese twists have their origin in West Africa. These braids are created using lin, synthetic material, kanekalon, or yarn extension material. It uses a two-strand braiding technique. Preplan the final style to determine how much material you will need. This will be determined by the length of the desired extension and the size of the partings. Separate and cut to the desired length.

To prepare the hair and scalp, shampoo, apply hot oil treatment, and blow dry. Match extension material to the hair color and texture.

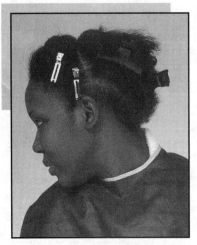

Part hair at 45-degree angle.

1. Start by dividing the entire head in half from ear to ear.
2. Slightly above the ear with tail of comb, make a 45-degree part down toward the neck. The part can be as large or small as required for the size of the twist you are trying to create.

3. Make a subsection above the ear. Separate the subsection into two equal parts. Section off a required amount of extension material. Place the extension strip between the two equal parts.
4. Simultaneously, you must perform two twisting motions. The first twisting is to roll the fiber between both of your fingers, which secures the natural hair into the fiber. The second twisting motion takes the "rolled" fiber and hair, and twists or overlaps one strand over the other. This rolling motion is done with the fingertip and should be very tight.

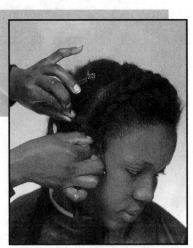

Roll fiber three or four times.

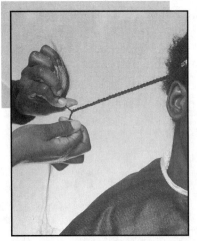

Twist one strand over the other to create a tight twist.

5. Continue the double twist motion for the entire length of the strand. Roll and cross strands until you reach the ends. Loop and knot the twists to close. Trim excess fiber.

Seal the ends in the predetermined fashion.

6. Seal ends with singeing method or knot and cut close.

Finished sealed ends

Diamond Casama Braids

Finished style

Casamas are created by using individual partings and braids that are larger in size than box braids or single braids. This technique requires three-strand braiding. The stitch of the braid itself is very tight, which allows the braid to curve when finished. The technique begins at the nape, where square, triangular, or rectangular partings are taken in any size desired. For the typical triangular style, triangles are one-half to one inch. The first two or three rows from the nape up can be horizontal; when you reach the top, preplan your design based on whether an asymmetrical look is desired or not. If it is, create a side part and plan to create braids that begin at the part line and move across the top of the head. This means the partings will follow an angled line and will not be perfectly horizontal at the top.

When the entire head is completed in the desired fashion, the free-hanging braids are singed with a burner. Senior braid stylist Fanta Kaba of Tendrils, New York, performs this technique.

1. Start in the back of the head by parting a diagonal section at about a 45-degree angle, toward the front hairline, just past the ear. This section can be from 1 to 2" wide.

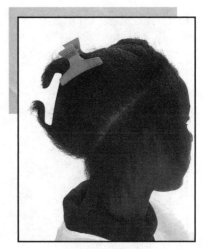

Part hair at 45-degree angle.

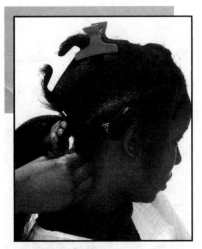

Diagonal subpartings

2. Part the base into subsections with vertical parts to create the diamond sections. After subsection size has been determined, select the appropriate amount of Kanekalon. For tapered ends, the extension material is gently pulled at both sides so that the ends have a "shredded," uneven effect.

3. Take a strand of synthetic hair in a predetermined length and fold it in half. Position the center of the strand at the base of the parting and wrap one half two or three revolutions around the base of the parted natural hair (base wrap is optional).

Three-strand braiding

"V" shape partings

4. Immediately divide the hair into three sections, with the natural hair encompassed into the center section. Make certain that the natural hair is concealed under the section before you begin three-strand braiding.

5. Alternate diagonal partings so that a "V" shape configuration is created in the back.

6. Partings should appear from front to back. Partings in front are curved and continue the diamond shape.

7. Braid the hair from scalp to ends, using an underhand or inverted technique. Each time you pass a side strand under the center strand, bring the center strand over tightly, so that the side strand becomes the new center strand. Then pass the alternate side strand under this one.

8. When you reach the ends, pull out a long, small section of hair, wrap it around the braid, knot it and repeat wrapping and knotting. This holds the tight braid in place and allows it to curve. Then continue to the next parting and repeat the entire procedure. Move up on the head, taking partings according to the preplanned design.

9. When the entire head is completed, you can heat-seal the ends.

Front to back partings

Braid Tapering

The beauty of the casama braid is that the braid is full and wide at the base and tapered off at the ends. The tapered ends usually have a slight curve. To create this effect, the extension material must be shed before applying it to the head.

1. Hold the required amount of extension material with two hands, about 6 to 10" apart.

2. Slowly pull the hair extension until it becomes uneven at the ends. By staggering at the ends, the extension material loses its blunt edges.

3. When staggering or redistributing extension material in an uneven manner, be aware of the length and size of the braid.

Cornrows and Senegalese Twist (Combo)

Finished style

This classic combination of micro cornrows and small Senegalese twists was sculpted by Avion Julien of Tulani's Regal Movement of New York.

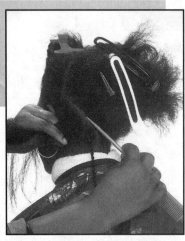

Senegalese twist back—45-degree angle

Diagonal parting

Part One

1. Start in the back by making a diagonal 45-degree-angle section to just above the client's ear. Part off a subsection by making a smaller vertical part to the bottom of the neck.

2. Divide the subsection into two equal parts.

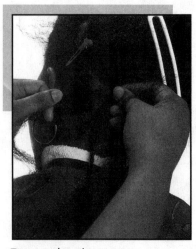

Two equal partings

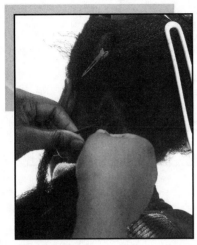

Hold and twist.

3. Double twist motion—roll hair strands counterclockwise.

4. Once the extension is twisted close to the scalp, cross over the two twisted strands. The roll-over-lap-roll sequence must be repeated for the entire twist. Tension must be consistent so that the twist remains straight.

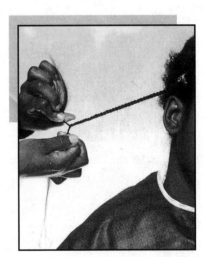

Create a tight braid.

Loop to close.

5. To close, loop ends by separating small numbers of strands and wrapping them around the braid. Singe ends secure and seal at the desired length.

Complete loop.

Trim.

6. Trim frizzies or split ends from the twist to complete finished style.

Part Two—Cornrow Front with Extension

1. Start at the hairline by parting off the base in the desired size. Vertical parts should be about 1/4" wide.

2. Divide the base into three equal portions. Take a premeasured strip of extension proportionately less than the size of the base. Using the feed-in method, apply small units of extension (ten to twenty hairs) to the hairline.

Pick up hair from the base and add to strand.

3. Begin the cornrow method. Each time you cross a strand from the outside to the inside center strand, pick up natural hair from the base and add it to the new center strand.

4. With your middle finger, hold the revolution in place. A second strip of extension can be added again to the left and outside strand.

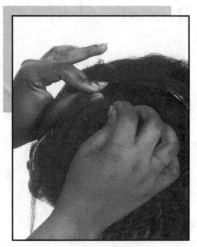

Hold the revolution in place.

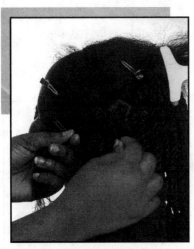

Create two equal portions.

5. After the cornrow base is completed, start the Senegalese twist motion by separating the center strand and adding it to the outside pieces, creating two equal portions.

6. Continue by starting the double twist motion in order to create the Senegalese twist.

7. Continue until you reach the end. Loop close, trim, and singe ends.

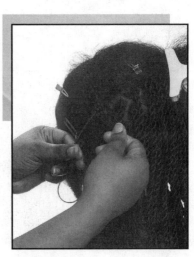

Roll and twist.

INDIVIDUAL BRAIDS

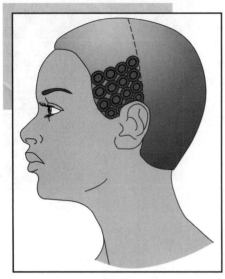

Twist or single braids placement

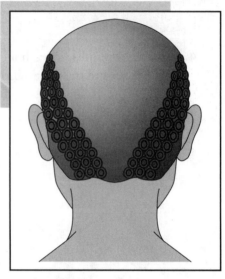

Twist or single braids placement—parting, sectioning, units

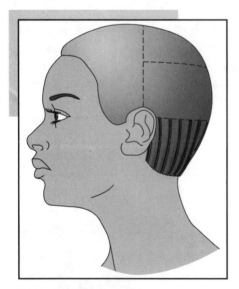

Cornrow—sectioning, parting

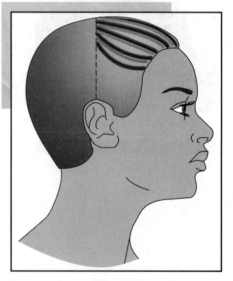

Cornrow placement—parting, sectioning

Individual braids may also be known as single or box braids. These are the most versatile to wear and they are directional—able to move or sweep into updos.

Whether you use human or synthetic extension or yarn, the variations of the braid are unlimited. Individual braids are traditional and classic. They are as fundamental as cornrows. Skill and practice are necessary in order to master this technique. The individual braid is a three-strand braid that, if done improperly, can create excessive tension and lead to breakage.

TIP!

The secrets to an excellent single braid are:

1. *The three portions are equal in size (uniform).*
2. *The braid is consistent and taut.*
3. *The braid is straight.*
4. *The base of the braid does not have a large loop or knot, putting excessive tension on the natural hair.*
5. *The braid must be tightly woven but done without pain to the client.*
6. *Parts should be consistent. As you get to the hairline, braids should be parted to camouflage any thin areas. This can be done using angled or brick-layered parts.*

Individual Braid

Finished style (shown with Diva Crimp enhancement)

Braid stylist Susan Bishop of Jaha Studio in Silver Springs, MD, uses this technique for the individual braid style.

1. Part the hair in half from ear to ear.

2. With diagonal partings from behind the ear to the nape of the neck, create a subsection with a vertical part for the base size of the braid. Take a predetermined amount of human hair to begin the braid.

3. Within that subsection, separate the hair into three equal parts.

Three equal portions

Secure, rotate, overlap, secure.

4. The braid revolution must include the client's natural hair. Each braid is created with the three-strand braid technique in which the strand on the side is always passed under the center strand.

5. Continue the braiding sequence with the outer strand crossing under to become the new center strand. Braid the human hair extension about 2" past the client's natural length. This helps to create fullness.

6. Trim the braid shaft for a finished look.

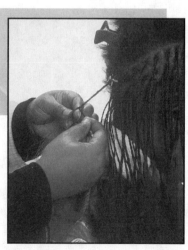

Braid extension two inches past the natural length for fullness

Diva Crimps

Creating the crimped texture to braids is an enhancement that has become very popular. It creates dimension and fullness without bulk. It helps to soften the braided style. Many people prefer this look because it gives the braids a loose, directional hair effect.

1. After the human hair extension is braided and the entire head is complete with braids, lightly spray mist to the whole length of the braid with a diluted setting mixture.

2. Saturate the braid enough to cover the entire depth of the braid. It should not be dripping wet, however, because that will increase the drying time.

3. Rebraid the braids. Take about six braids, divide them into three sets (about two braids per section) and braid from the base to the very end. Roll this rebraided hair on to a roller, using a pink or blue perm rod (small).

4. Allow to dry thoroughly.

5. Unbraid the braided strands. Be careful not to disturb the braided extension.

6. Use fingers to take out the double braid. (Flip rebraided hair on the underside and proceed to unravel the braids with an underhand braiding motion.)

7. Trim and shape any uneven ends. The single braids should appear curly and texturized.

Geni-Locs

Finished style

Geni-Locs is a style that uses yarn as an extension. It is one of the hairlocking alternatives that offers the benefit and beauty of locks without committing to locks permanently. They are versatile and can be bent and twisted into many different shapes to adorn the face. The Geni-Loc involves a braid-wrap technique to accomplish its finished look.

This technique is a specialty of braid designer Debra Hare-Bey of Red Creative Salon in New York.

Pull out two pieces for wrap.

1. Cut yarn at least twice the desired finished length. Give yourself enough length because the yarn must be folded before adding to natural hair.

2. Separate four predetermined sizes of hair to start the first braid. Loop two pieces of yarn within the two pieces; then divide into three equal portions.

3. Begin the braid by placing looped pieces of extension on the three equal strands of natural hair. After the second revolution, pull out two pieces of yarn from the center for the wrapping. Continue to braid with the remaining pieces. Four pieces still remain, leaving one piece for the left strand 1, two pieces for the center strand 2, and one piece for the right strand 3.

4. Braid down the entire length.

5. Hold the braid close to the base with your left hand. Take two free pieces and begin to wind under and around the braid. With each revolution, move slightly down the braid so that the yarn does not overlap.

6. Continue the wrapping movement until the ends are reached. Braid ends closed. Trim the braid shaft to complete the braid style.

7. Singe braided ends and mold with fingers. Cut singed ends to remove excess material. Reburn if necessary to shape ends.

8. The front is parted on the diagonal for the design and to create fullness.

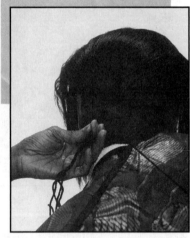

Wrap yarn under and around entire braid.

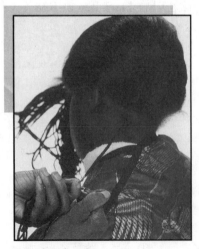

Singe braid ends.

Front diagonal part

The Afro "Congo Crown"

Finished style

Afros are back! They are fun, versatile, and can be extended to any color, length, or shape. The Afro weave adds a new dimension to textured hairstyling. This weave can be done with synthetic hair, human hair, or yak and human hair blends. The look is as contemporary today as it was in the 1960s. Weaving in hair can protect natural hair that has been chemically damaged. It covers balding or thinning spots, allowing the natural hair to grow.

The style that is featured in this section uses a yak and human hair blend. This blend offers a look that is close to natural. It is soft, yet the texture is very tight and coily. It is a customized blend that is sewn on a weft (hair sewn together to create a single line edge or strip.) The weft will be sewn onto a **track** (cornrows designed into a pattern for the foundation to place a weave extension).

| NOTE! | *When adding extensions, color and texture must match natural hair. When using a spiral synthetic hair for the finished look, separate each spiral curl for a fuller, curly style.* |

Parting small base—circular pattern

1. Measure and separate 1 to 2" of the natural hairline around the entire head. Clamp away or braid down the hairline to separate it from the loose hair during the process. (You can do this with one large cornrow around the hairline.) Follow the natural hairline and begin the foundation for the weave by parting a small base in a circular pattern around the head to begin a small cornrow track.

2. Cornrow in a circular pattern twice around the head. Keep cornrows flat and thin to avoid bulk. At the top of the crown, start a zig-zag pattern down the head. Keep within the circle. Extend cornrows past the length of the hair.

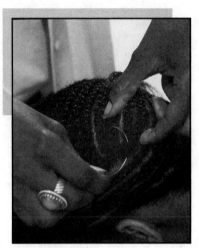

Zig-zag pattern

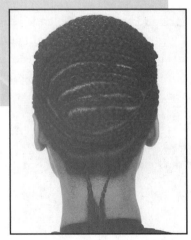

Fold and sew.

3. Once the foundation or track has been laid, take the excess braid that is not on the scalp, fold it onto the track at the crown of the head, and sew it or attach it.

4. With all the ends folded, sewn, and tucked away, the hair is ready for the wefted extension.

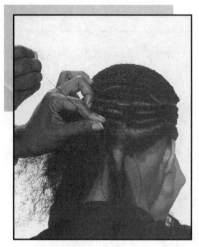

Needle through weft

5. With a double-loop "lock-in" stitch, attach the weft to the cornrowed track. Pull the needle through the weft and the bottom of the braid as you secure the track with your opposite hand. Pull the needle up until a small loop remains, then insert the needle twice through the loop and pull it tight.

6. Follow the cornrow track around the head by positioning loops about 1/4" apart. Continue until the entire track is placed and secure the ends by inserting the needle through the loop three or four times.

Track around head

Secure track and complete.

7. Continue to sew and loop with the premeasured track for the zig-zag section of the head.

8. Once the weave is secure, open up the loose cornrow that you first made around the hairline. Then, incorporate the natural hair with the extension. Hair may be set on perm rods to add texture and curl.

Pixie Braids

Finished style

The pixie braid style offers a youthful, short braid look. These individual braids are usually small to medium in size. The braids are layered to various lengths, usually framing the face. It is best to use a Kanekalon synthetic hair because this fiber singes better when molding the tips. The ends are cut and singed closed for the desired length.

The pixie braid must be tight. This will create a curved braid. There should be a light, airy feel to the braids. The layers create the feathered look by singeing the tips wherever necessary to complete the style. Your hair must be short for this technique and the finished braid can be slightly longer than the natural length. The braid is singed 1 to 2" longer than your natural hair.

1. Follow steps of individual braid instruction to start pixie braids.

2. Maintain the three-strand, outside-to-inside strand underhand braiding technique. Keep the braid stitch close.

Three-strand braid sequence

3. To hold the tight stitch taut, double loop the ends. Bring together the three strands; hold in one hand. With the other hand, separate several strands away from the braid, loop over and around, and pull through the loop. Repeat.

First loop

Second loop

4. Trim directly under the knot. Singe the knot to close. The singed ends will be warm and soft enough to mold by rolling the melted synthetic fiber between thumb and finger. This will give the ends a sharp, pointed, neat finish.

Trim.

Flat Twists

Finished style

Flat twists are a great alternative for people with medium to shoulder-length hair. These twists are regal, soft, and easily sculpted into a day or evening look. Flat twists are a wonderful option for women interested in wearing their hair natural, but who do not want extensions or a woven braided look. Whether the hair is relaxed or chemical free, this sculpted style offers an elegant and sophisticated crown of glory.

The flat twist is a two-strand, flat-on-the-scalp braid. The pattern resembles a flat spiral on a candy cane. Master braider Cecelia Hinds of Uzuri Braids in Washington, D.C. uses this technique. Two strands of equal proportions are twisted onto the scalp, picking up natural hair with every revolution. Most flat twist styles can last for two to three weeks.

To maintain this style, no shampooing is required. Cover nightly with a satin scarf. Oil scalp as needed.

"Lin Twist"—Flat Twist with Lin

Finished style

Lin twists are the new classic to updo braiding styles. They give medium to shoulder-length hair dimension and diversity. The style can last three to four weeks. It can be done in two hours and is a quick alternative for women who want extensions incorporated into their braid style. This technique also has been mastered by Cecelia Hinds of Uzuri Braids.

Lin twist—side

1. The two-strand twist can be performed by the roll-and-twist method at the hairline. Place the lin flat on top of the two equal portions. Secure the lin to each base with the double twist sequence, picking up natural hair with each revolution.

2. The style should contour with your head along the sides and back.

3. Gather the extended ends into a french roll or inverted cornrow; pin and tuck.

Lin twist—back

Silky Twist

Finished style

This flat twist is stately and majestic and is featured by master braider N'gone Sow of Soween Braids in New York. The silky twist is intricate yet quick and easy. This style was created by laying the synthetic hair or lin flat onto equal portions of natural hair. The hair was parted into sections about the size of a large cornrow base.

A roll-twist motion secures the fiber. This preplanned design is parted into a sculpted updo and rolled in the back. The extension chignon on top is gelled, pinned, and then sewn to secure the rolled and looped strands.

This rolled twist requires little maintenance. Oil the scalp once or twice per week and cover the braided style nightly.

Silky Wrap

Silky wrap

The silky wrap is an exotic and intricate braid style. This style, mastered by free-lance hair designer Susan Hale of New York, is created with synthetic hair. First, the hair is braided into a desired length and is then wrapped with an extended strip of hair. This wrapping of synthetic hair gives the braid its glossy look. Excessive winding can be uncomfortable; be aware of the stress around the hairline. After the wrapping process, the braid can be molded and shaped. Ends are singed closed. This style may last up to two months.

Silky Wrap and Goddess Braids

Goddess braid/silky wrap

This combination of braid techniques is alluring and provocative. The large inverted goddess braid lays flat on the scalp in a predesigned sculpted pattern. Cecelia Hinds of Uzuri Braids creates this style. The extended braid is swept to the crown giving it height and dimension. The silk wrap frames the face and tendril over one eye.

CHAPTER 7

Natural Style Options

AFROS, COIL-TWISTS, AND LOCKS

The current popularity of chemical-free, natural, or virgin hair is no fad, but is a movement toward redefining what is beautiful, acceptable, and emotionally rewarding for people with textured hair. The vicious cycle of relaxing-braiding-relaxing has stopped for many women. Remember: Everything we do is a statement about self. From what we eat to how we wear our hair, how we see and feel about ourselves is reflected. The world will have its own definition about that reflection, but you must be clear and have convictions that make up your inner being—your soul.

The natural hair-care specialist can be a liberator of souls. By helping you to redefine how you see yourself, giving you more options to beauty enhancement products, and reinforcing the styling options with nurturing regular support, your hair specialist frees you from stereotypical hairstyles and allows you to be you. This empowers and builds self-esteem.

Katherine Jones, president of IBN (International Braiders Network), during a phone interview with the author, agrees: "The one word that natural hair-care clients use unanimously to describe the many advantages to natural hair styles is . . . freedom! Freedom to think about and participate in a variety of rewarding activities because they are no longer chained to their hair. When a woman is at peace with her hair, she is at peace with herself and the world."

Braids and extensions are a large part of African history. Today, these traditional African hair-care methods have re-emerged as an essential component to bringing one closer to one's natural hair. Extensions are transitional in that they are a means to maintain one's natural hair.

After you have worn braids for several years, the most basic step is to remove the extensions and "go natural." This means that you are ready to welcome and surrender to your texture, kink, nap, or coil. The natural hair-care specialist can help you to change perspective and accept genetic inheritance.

There are Afros, coil-twists, and the ultimate of natural hair—the lock. Variations of these styles are endless and, for the future, we will see men and women opting to wear these textured styles. It does not matter whether your hair is textured or not; the redefining of our cultural aesthetics frees everyone, even those stylists that define beauty with more European standards.

The following natural styles offer you an opportunity to finally accept your hair.

Blow Out

Finished style

The "blow out" is a blown dried Afro. The heat from the blow dryer elongates the hair, giving it a longer, fuller look. Avoid excessive heat and pulling when blow drying.

1. After hair is blown dry, divide the hair into four to six sections from the nape of the neck to the occipital bone. Hair clip or twist away to separate sections.

Divide hair into four to six sections.

Establish guideline.

2. To trim ends 1/4", use the first section as a guide. Hold a 1" subsection down with hand in line with horizontal parting. Cut to the desired length. This establishes your design guideline.

3. Move up the head and part off a 1/2" vertical section. Bring first guideline into this vertical section, connect lengths, and cut. This creates the design for the length side. Continue upward after every new section for the desired look.

4. To create uniform layers with textured hair, use guidelines to maintain shape and length. For the top, hold the 1" section at a 90-degree angle (straight up) and cut straight across. Comb into the sides and the back guideline and connect lengths.

5. Use a pick or large-tooth comb to comb out hair. Comb or pick to make sure hair is distributed evenly. Stand back and observe your work from a distance; make certain the weight of the hair is properly distributed for the desired style.

6. Repeat the procedure until the cut is entirely even. Spray with oil sheen to finish the style.

Vertical guideline.

The African Kurl (Twist Out)

Finished style

The basic "blow out" previously shown was transformed into textured tresses that can be worn at the office or for an evening out. It softly flows and bounces to all the urban beats.

The African kurl is wonderful because it can be offered as a service for more than one style.

1. The hair is double twisted on the individual braid pattern. This is a double twist set—the hair is wet and sprayed with a setting lotion.

2. After the hair is totally dry, you can wear this twist style for two or three weeks. Oil the scalp sparingly once or twice a week.

3. After a week or two, if you want to change the style, untwist the twists. We call it "twist out." The "twist out" can be done on the same day of the set for a beautiful, fresh look. Some people opt to wait one to two weeks before opening the twist in order to add versatility and long life to the crimped tresses.

4. Separate each twist for a full, bountiful look. Avoid disturbing the wave pattern. Use fingers to fan out the twist. A small pick can be used to remove parts and to lift. Only use a pick at the base of the scalp. This will last two to three weeks. Use moisturizing sheen when necessary.

5. This set can also be applied to relaxed, straight hair. Drying time is one hour and perm rods can be used for a spiral, fuller effect.

The Short Afro

Finished style

The short Afro for women is created by a free form of cutting curly hair using a clipper and a large comb. The hair is graduated from the perimeter up and is cut to work with the head shape. Naeemah Jeff of 'Locks 'N Chops' Natural Hair Salon in New York uses the following technique, in which the hair is cut when it is dry.

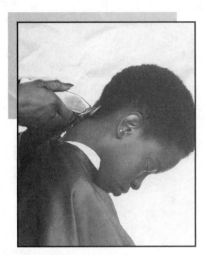

Cut the first quarter inch.

1. First pick the hair out, using a jumbo comb with wide-set teeth. Observe its density closely—particularly if you do not want much of the scalp to show through. Extremely curly hair gives the illusion that it is cut close. You will not see the scalp, but density counts most when deciding how close to cut the hair. In this instance , only the first 1/2" at the nape and sides is cut so close that some of the scalp shows through.

2. Begin at the nape and cut the first 1/4", using a clipper-over-comb technique. Place the comb flat against the head.

3. Move to the next section, smoothly bringing the comb upward and cutting again. Observe the first 1/2" to make certain that the hair is as close or as far away from the scalp as you want it.

4. Continue cutting in this manner, working with the head shape. About 1" up the head, begin graduating the cut. Use the angle of the comb to do this. Angle the comb slightly away from the head as you cut, and continue working up the back of the head. Rotate the tips of the comb toward the head as you lift the hair to create graduation. Work with a smooth, flowing motion, inserting the comb and working across sections, then moving up. (Avoid jerky movements.)

5. When you reach the occipital, stand back and observe your work at a distance to make certain the weight is properly distributed. (If you observe your work from too close a vantage point, you could be fooled into thinking the shape is cleaner than it actually is.)

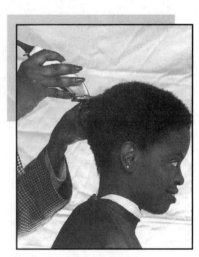

Angle the comb and cut.

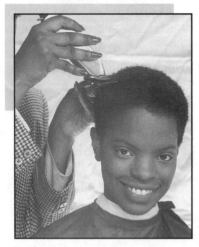

Graduate the hair.

6. Next move to the sides and repeat this procedure to cut the first 1/2" or so very close to the head. Then angle the comb to graduate the hair and work to the top of the head. Repeat this procedure on the opposite side.

7. To complete the cut, lift the front hairline and cut it freehand with the clippers. Then dampen the dry hair and add a liquid polish styling product.

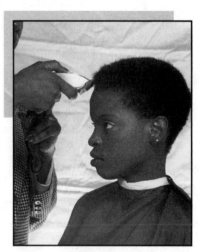

Cut the front hairline.

African Kurl and Flat Twist "Sunburst"

Finished style

This combination of natural twist is fresh and youthful. The styles mix a curly look with the sculpted flat twist that spreads sunshine to every face. The tighter the coil pattern, the more texture the curls will have. These curls are versatile and can last for up to six weeks.

For more fullness and volume, a twist out service can be offered. You can untwist both the kurls and the flat twist for styling options.

Four sections

1. Shampoo and deep condition the hair. Towel dry, squeezing out excess moisture. Hair should be damp but not dripping wet.

2. With tail comb, divide the hair in half from ear to ear. Then divide the back portion of the hair into four sections.

3. Beginning at the nape, lightly apply a pinch of water-soluble gel to each subsection. With a horizontal parting, subdivide vertically 1/4" partings. Overlap equal portions counterclockwise and two-strand twist to the ends of the strand. The twist must be tight, so revolutions should be close together to form the curl pattern.

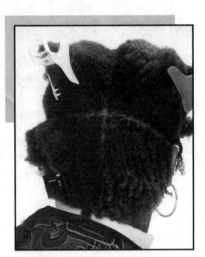

Close together to form curl

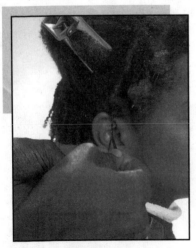

4. When the back is completed, move to the side and repeat the twist movement.

5. Dampen hair in front with a spray bottle of water and oil to keep moist. Flat twist damp hair into a small, sculpted pattern. Place under dryer until completely dry.

6. Lightly oil scalp and finish with moisturizing spray sheen.

Lower side two strands

Nubian Coils

Styling the hair in Nubian coils is the first step toward locking hair. Nubian coils are small spiral-formed curls usually short to medium in length. The texture of the hair determines the formation or coil pattern. Some coil patterns are tighter or closer together than others. If the coil pattern is smaller, then the coil will be tight. The reverse also holds true: the larger the wave or curl formation, the larger in size the actual coil will be. By examining the coil pattern of several strands of hair over the entire head, you will be able to determine the size and characteristics of the coil formation.

To examine the hair for coil pattern, check three different areas of the head:

1. The nape (the "kitchen") is usually tight, very coily or curly, and dense.

2. The side hairline is usually slightly less coily or curly and may be thinner or finer in density. Look for damage or alopecia.

3. The crown may have the least curl or wave pattern. For some menopausal women, this area may thin and bald. However, this area is usually rich with a dense capacity of hair.

The average person has several textures of hair from gray wiry to fine coily. Be aware of the differences and apply the necessary techniques based on the hair texture to get the best results before locking.

Nubian coils are the "prelock phase" before African locks or dreadlocks, as they are often called. This prelocked phase is a beautiful style in itself and can be worn to work or for play. It is neat yet at the same time loose in structure. When done initially, Nubian coils are flat and contoured to the head. By using different styling gels, a shiny/glossy glow gives the coils their finished look. However, after about forty-eight hours, the coil "puffs" open slightly—just enough to expand the spiral and soften the curl. The coil formation is still in place and can last for up to six weeks. The life of this coiled style depends on the size of the coil. Smaller coils last longer and the tighter the coil or curl pattern, the longer the style will last because this style is the preparatory style for African locks.

The person that is interested in locking is at a high commitment level, physically, emotionally, and spiritually willing to invest the time—usually six months to a year—for the locks to solidify and mature.

Hairlocking is a natural coiling process of textured curly hair without the use of combs or chemicals. The hair meshes and spirals within itself, interlocking and adhering until the joined strands become a tight, dense unit or lock. The hair locks in slow developmental stages, which can take anywhere from six months to a year depending on the length, density, and coil pattern. Cultivating locks is a process, a journey into self-discovery and acceptance of our genetic and cultural inheritance.

There are several ways to cultivate locks such as double twisting, wrapping with cord or wire, braiding with or without extension, or simply not disturbing the hair by not combing or brushing the lock (like the Rastafarians of Jamaica do)—by just leaving the hair to its own natural course, the hair will lock. However, it will not have a groomed, manicured look. These type of locks can be called "organic" locks. Cultivated African locks have symmetry and balance. The goal to grooming locks is to create uniform tresses that will turn heads when well groomed. Symmetry is not easy to accomplish with textured hair. Although the hair is programmed genetically to coil, no two coils are exactly alike. It is the lock-tician's responsibility to develop a system that promotes symmetry into the textured hair. Three basic methods of locking are: (1) comb technique; (2) palm roll, and (3) braid or extension.

The most effective techniques that use the natural coil pattern are the comb technique and the palm roll method. The comb technique can be most effective during the early stages of locking while the coil is still open. This method of coiling entails placing the comb at the base and, in a rotating motion, spiraling the hair into a curl. With each revolution the comb moves down until it reaches the end of the hair shaft. It offers a great tight coil and is excellent on short (1 to 3") hair.

The second method of grooming and starting locks is the palm roll method. This method is the gentlest on the hair and guides it through all the natural stages of locking. Palm rolling takes advantage of the hair's natural ability to coil. The following description shows how to use the palm roll method to create a coiled style.

Nubian Coils—Prelocking Phase

1. To begin, shampoo and condition the hair. Then towel blot the hair, squeezing out excess moisture so that the hair is damp but not wet.

2. Next part the hair in horizontal rows from the nape all the way to the front hairline. Then divide the first horizontal row at the nape into equal-sized subsections. The subsections can be square, circular, triangular, or rectangular; the size of the individual sections and their shape depends on the desired finished look. Before palm rolling, use the hair clips to hold the hair around the subsection out of the way.

3. Beginning at the nape on the far side, take the hair within the first subsection and lightly apply a pinch of gel, using your right forefinger and thumb. Then pinch the hair near the scalp and twist it one full counterclockwise revolution. (If you are left-handed, use your left hand to pinch the hair, but always turn it counterclockwise.)

Palm rolling

4. With one smooth motion, pass the hair from your right hand to your left hand, tuck the hair into the recession near the thumb and fold your thumb down to hold the hair in place. Position your left hand behind your right hand so that the left fingertips are at the right wrist. Slide your right hand back while simultaneously sliding the hand forward.

5. When the hair is between your palms, pull out your thumb so that the hair is rolled between your palms. When the fingertips of your right hand are near the left-hand wrist, fold your thumb back down to recapture the hair.

Nubian coils with yarn extension

6. So that the hair is always rolled in a counterclockwise direction, reposition the left hand behind the right hand and repeat the palm rolling technique. Each time you roll the hair, move progressively down the hair shaft. When you reach the ends, place the lock down neatly and begin again with the adjacent subsection.

7. When each subsection in the first horizontal row has been completed, move up to the next horizontal row and subdivide it as before. If you rolled the previous subsections from right to left, this time work from left to right. Continue this pattern all the way to the crown. As you work up the head, include the side sections. Always maintain a degree of moisture by using the spray bottle as needed. Also, apply the same amount of gel to each subsection.

8. When you reach the crown, continue palm rolling subsections, directing them to move toward the back. When you reach the top of the head, move around to accommodate the desired finished style. The front can be individualized, for instance, with few sections moved onto the forehead.

9. When all the hair has been palm rolled, dry the hair completely, but no more than necessary, under a hood dryer set on low heat.

10. When the hair is completely dry, finish the style by applying a light oil to add sheen.

11. Single braids with yarn are a lock alternative that is added to the front to frame the face. The ends are looped and singed to the desired length.

African Locks

The ultimate in natural hair care is the textured richness of hairlocking. Throughout the continent of Africa various tribes have practiced this art form and cultural expression of beauty enhancement. The people of the Pokot, Massai, Mau Mau, Kau, Ashanti, and Fulani, as well as many others, practice some form of locking. Some tribes use mud or a red clay with straw or hay to perform the grooming technique.

Locks symbolize what the Afro was in the 1960s: a symbol of freedom, cultural empowerment, and identity, as well as a seed to self-acceptance. Ona Osirio-Maat, a locktician for eleven years, is the creator of the **LockSmyth method,** a lock technique that incorporates a special, rhythmical palm rolling technique. Osirio-Maat states during a phone interview with the author, "Locked hair is the ultimate natural hair statement. It says you have come home . . . finally. The self-love and appreciation that has been gained from 'growing' through the process can have tremendous transformative power surrounding the 'locker' life. People usually undergo some deeper level of self-evaluation as they return for professional cultivation of their locks, and the stories center around their hair getting longer and stronger. Also, there are stories about the strength their locks silently display. As a locktician, I witness the internal growth of my clients as well as the inches of hair flowing down their backs. Their pride is tempered by the humility of the process. Instead of running fast, hard, and long distances from the kink, they changed their perspective and began to embrace the coil."

DEVELOPMENTAL STAGES OF HAIRLOCKING

Depending on the coil pattern, density, and length of hair, the locking process may vary from six to twelve months to lock the entire head.

Phase I. Prelock Stage—Hair is soft and is coiled into spiral configurations. The coil is smooth and the end is open. The coil has a shiny or a glossy texture.

Phase II. Sprouting Stage—Hair begins to interlace and mesh. The separate units begin to "puff up" and expand in size. The units are no longer glossy, thin, and smooth. Little bulbs or knots form at the middle or ends of the coiled unit indicating that the coil is starting to close. This "plumping" of the lock may give the head an unkempt look. Avoid overgrooming or excessive twisting at this phase. The length starts to shrink because the coil is solidifying. This "frizzy" look is part of the process. Here is where patience and desire are a virtue—and the level of commitment is tested. This is also the stage in which some sections of the head will be totally locked while other portions of the head will still have soft and open coils. Be aware of the different coil patterns and density of the hair in these specific areas.

Phase III. Growing Stage—The hair strands adhere to one another, creating a network of tresses within each coiled unit. Interlacing and meshing can be felt by squeezing the lock. You can feel a bulb at the end of each lock. The locking process starts at the middle or ends of the unit, not at the scalp. Hair begins to regain length. The lock still may be frizzy yet solid in some areas. Locks are closed at the ends, dense, and dull, not reflecting light to get any sheen.

> **NOTE!** *Textured, curly, coily hair does not reflect light the way straight hair does. This dullness or the lack of luster is part of the process and is what creates the lock. One can add oils that allow the light to reflect off the oils and give the hair a gloss.*

Phase IV. Maturation Stage—The lock is now totally closed at the end. The unit is interlaced and meshed and in contrast to the size, giving the hair a tighter, rope-like look except where there is new growth at the base. The network of inter-twined strands is tight and hard to the touch. The hair grows at a rapid rate. Whether the strands are in the **anagen cycle** or **telogen** cycle of growth, all the hair is fused together; because the hair is not combed or brushed, there is little shedding. The hair stays within the locked unit. New sprouts spring up between mature locks. In some cases, the hair forms whole new locks.

> **NOTE!** *Some textures will not close at the end. A single curl or wave may exist at the end of the lock, giving the lock the appearance of being open. The maturation stage will still continue.*

Phase V. Atrophy Stage—After several years of maturation (the usual time varies between seven and ten years) the lock may start to weaken or atrophy at the ends. The smaller the lock, the more fragile and more likely the atrophy will occur. The larger the lock, the more durable it is and the degeneration may never occur. This atrophy stage usually occurs at the nape of the neck and around the frontal and peripheral hairlines. When the hair starts to weaken, make sure it is part of a natural locking process and not due to physical or emotional stress. How to tell the difference:

1. Thinning and breakage at the ends is a degenerative process and part of the locks' life cycle; excessive dryness and texture can accelerate this process.
2. Thinning and breakage at the base or scalp is the body's warning signal that something is internally or externally imbalanced.

HOW TO CULTIVATE AND GROOM LOCKS

There is an effective seven-step procedure for grooming and cultivating locks:

1. To start locks, use the palm roll technique described earlier in the chapter.
2. Avoid overtwisting. With each revolution move down the shaft to avoid overspiraling the hair.
3. During the first three months, have the locks groomed every three or four weeks.
4. Grooming may entail:
   - herbal shampoo
   - hot oil treatment
   - herbal rinse or acid rinse
   - rerolling, cultivating, or manicuring
   - trim (optional)

- styling (texturizing to include crimping, curling, braiding, and so on)
- watering: spritzing locks with water helps keep locks or natural curls clean. The weight of water helps the lock drop down in length and brings lint to the surface. Keeping locks wet is one of the keys to growth and promotes the natural curling of hair.

5. Always remove lock debris, lint, and excess oils embedded in locks.

6. Avoid using heavy petroleum or waxy oils. Use diluted moisturizing and water-soluble gels when rolling the hair.

7. Once the locks are fully matured, the hair can be shampooed more often.

CAUTION! *Be careful not to dry out the hair. Use lemon rinses and acid rinses to loosen the lock debris after each shampoo for deep cleansing. Follow with light, hot oil treatments to the scalp.*

Locked hair may appear dull, lackluster, or drab when not properly cared for. Locks do, however, have a beautiful sheen and luster when healthy and clean. The sheen is subtly understated and soft because, like most natural fibers, locks have a matte finish; this finish is a part of their natural beauty and uniqueness. Avoid applying large amounts of braid oil or moisturizing sheen to create more shine; this contributes to lock sediment build-up. Once or twice a week, small amounts of natural oil (dime-size) can be applied to the scalp and massaged through the hair to create luster. With locks, "less is more."

STYLING AND TEXTURIZING LOCKS

At the salon Tendrils in Brooklyn, NY, texture is used to enhance the natural tress. The finer the lock, the more versatility you will have to create new looks. Avoid putting too much stress on the hair to eliminate breakage. Remember: Thin locks are fragile.

Finished Style

■ Texturizing—On damp locks, lightly spray a setting lotion. Braid or twist the entire length. Add a perm rod or clip to hold the end. The hair must be completely dry before unbraiding or twisting out in order to get style.

■ Tendrils/Spirals—On damp locks, lightly spray a setting lotion to the entire lock surface. With a perm rod (pink, purple, or white), vertically wind the lock around the rod, starting at the end of the hair and moving up toward the scalp.

■ Updo Sweeps—Roll, twist, braid, pin, and tuck. Create chignons, buns, french rolls, and inverted braids—be as creative as your hair will let you. There are no limits!

Unswept locks—side

MATERIALS FOR EXTENSIONS

There are a variety of materials that are available for the purpose of extending textured hair. The life of the style, however, will always be determined by the materials used. As braid extensions become more popular, more varieties of quality and price will be available. Though it may save money to buy the least expensive product, especially if you buy in large quantities, beware that you may not get the desired results. In other words, the extension material is critical to the final outcome of your hair design. When buying a new product, buy in small quantities and test the fiber on a mannequin.

The following list may help you to decide what extension material to use:

1. Kanekalon—This is a manufactured synthetic fiber of excellent quality. It is designed to have a texture similar to African hair types. It does not reflect light, which means it has less shine. It is durable and holds up to shampooing and styling. When braiding the hair, it is smooth to the scalp and fingers, which is very important because it does not cut or damage natural hair as other less expensive products do. It generally has a softer feel and tangles less than other synthetics. It comes in a variety of colors. It is versatile and easy to match with natural hair colors. Kanekalon costs more than most synthetics but is a better quality—not only according to manufacturers but also according to many braid stylists. This extension material finishes well when using the singeing method; it burns safely and seals quickly.

2. Nylon/Rayon Synthetic—This product is less expensive and readily available. The quality can vary depending on the brand name. You must be familiar with the brands in order to get a decent quality. In general, the less expensive synthetic hair tangles more and can damage natural hair. Nylon and rayon have been known to cut or break the hair. They are often less durable after repeated shampooing. They also reflect light and leave hair very shiny. You must be cautious when choosing the quality of the extension material. Nylon and rayon synthetics, however, come in more varieties of color than Kanekalon. However, these materials do not burn well when using the singe method to close synthetic extensions. The warm plastic melts too quickly, holds heat, and can burn and blister the skin.

NOTE! *It has been my experience that when the hair is shampooed regularly, the natural hair begins to expand, but the Kanekalon or synthetic hair does not. As the natural hair expands, the tension at the base of the braid with the extension increases.*

CAUTION! *Warning: Nylon and rayon synthetic material finishes poorly when using the singeing method; melted fibers can stick to the skin and burn. Avoid nylon and rayon when singeing.*

3. Human Hair—This material is the most confusing of fibers and is somewhat mysterious. Most of the product is imported from Asia. It is a closed market, and very little is known about how the human hair is produced or processed. Some of it is imported from Europe and small amounts are from Africa. Although the label may say human hair, buyer beware—all that glitters is not gold. The buyer must select hair from a reputable dealer or a wholesaler of this product to be assured of its quality. Prepackaged human hair is generally less expensive than that which is customized by a wholesaler. If a wholesaler is not available in your area, consider mail order. This material (supposedly) is derived from human hair and is processed into hundreds of colors and textures. It is versatile, soft, and tangle free. Although the material is extremely expensive, sometimes overpriced, it moves and feels like natural hair. It expands along with human hair when it is washed, which may also change the desired results and the life of a particular hairstyle. It can easily slip from the base of the braid. But unlike Kanekalon, it can be reused, if properly cleaned and combed. This product is ideal for those who are allergic to the synthetic products. To finish braid styles with human hair, you can use thermal curling tools and set the hair for crimps.

4. Human Hair Weft—Wefted human hair has all the advantages of loose human hair, except that when it is shampooed it does not expand to the point that it can slip from the base. The material is sewn together on a woven strip that interlaces the individual human hair strands. Wefted human hair is a great alternative to add dimension, length, and color to natural hair. Wefted hair is sewn in with a needle and thread to a braided cornrow track and netting.

5. Yarn—Traditional yarn material is used to make fabric for sweaters, hats, and so on. But now it is being used to adorn textured African hair. When braided or wrapped, it is light, soft, and detangles easily. Yarn comes in many colors. The most commonly used is black or brown for a more natural look. It is different than synthetic fibers because it does not reflect any light. It is not glossy. It gives the braid style a matte finish and can give braids a "locked" look. But be careful when choosing yarns. Some black yarns have a blue or green tint. A yarn may appear jet black in the store but in the light it reflects green. Always hold yarn to the light before purchasing. It is very inexpensive and easy to find. Also, the yarn can be cotton or a nylon blend and though it may expand when shampooing, it does not slip from the base. So, braid styles are durable with yarns. Do not burn yarns if they are 100% cotton. Finish braids with a neat knot.

6. Lin—This is a beautiful wool fiber made in France and imported from Africa. Like yarn, it has a matte finish and gives off little shine. It comes only in black and brown. Lin can be purchased in packages of 25 meters or 24 yards. It comes on a roll and is used in any length and size. Often used for Senegalese twists and "Corkscrew" styles, this fiber cannot be singed. It is cottony and very flammable. Braid styles using lin are generally not shampooed often.

7. Yak—This strong textured fiber comes from the domestic ox, usually found in the mountains of Tibet and Central Asia. The hairs on the ox are long on the sides and the back. These hairs are shaved and processed to use alone or blended with human hair. The variety of blends usually creates a more African texture when yak is used in wigs. Small mixtures of yak with human hair helps to remove the manufactured shine.

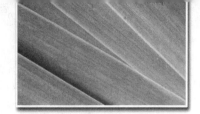

Index